Toilets that make Compost

Praise for the book ...

'Toilets that make compost is a truly excellent book, full of sound practical advice. I'm now convinced that in dispersed rural areas in developing countries the sanitation system of first choice is the *Arborloo*. Growing food trees and/or medicinal trees in full *Arborloo* pits raises people out of malnutrition and poverty. This sanitation system needs to be used much more widely and it will then make a substantial contribution to achieving the Millennium Development Goals.'

Professor Duncan Mara, University of Leeds, UK

'Rarely does a book come along that can change the world, but Toilets that Make Compost is one such book. For that half of the world that has no sanitation, this book is a gift. Peter Morgan has created simple ecological toilet designs that are inexpensive and easy to build and which create useful compost that increases plant productivity and the food security of poor families. The *Arborloo* toilet, created by Morgan, has taken off in Ethiopia with tens of thousands now in use and increasing each day. This book is highly recommended to agencies that want to make a difference in the world.'

Dr Mayling Simpson-Hebert, Catholic Relief Services, Nairobi, Kenya.

Toilets that make Compost
Low-cost, Sanitary Toilets that produce Valuable Compost for Crops in an African Context

Peter Morgan

Practical Action Publishing Ltd
27a Albert Street, Rugby, CV21 2SG, Warwickshire, UK
www.practicalactionpublishing.org

© Stockholm Environment Institute, 2008

First published by Stockholm Environment Institute, 2007

ISBN 13 Paperback: 9781853396748
ISBN Library Ebook: 9781780441313
Book DOI: http://dx.doi.org/10.3362/9781780441313

All rights reserved. No part of this publication may be reprinted or reproduced or utilized in any form or by any electronic, mechanical, or other means, now known or hereafter invented, including photocopying and recording, or in any information storage or retrieval system, without the written permission of the publishers.

A catalogue record for this book is available from the British Library.

The authors, contributors and/or editors have asserted their rights under the Copyright Designs and Patents Act 1988 to be identified as authors of their respective contributions.

Since 1974, Practical Action Publishing has published and disseminated books and information in support of international development work throughout the world. Practical Action Publishing is a trading name of Practical Action Publishing Ltd (Company Reg. No. 1159018), the wholly owned publishing company of Practical Action. Practical Action Publishing trades only in support of its parent charity objectives and any profits are covenanted back to Practical Action (Charity Reg. No. 247257, Group VAT Registration No. 880 9924 76).

Contents

Acknowledgements		vii
Figures		ix
1	Introduction	17
2	Compost-making toilets	19
	Arborloo – The simplest single pit compost toilet	20
	Fossa alterna – The double alternating pit compost toilet	20
3	*Arborloo* – The single pit compost toilet	23
	How to build the single pit compost toilet	25
	How to make ring beams	27
	Building the toilet house (superstructure)	34
	Making an Arborloo fitted with a pedestal	35
	Types of superstructure	38
	How to use the single pit compost toilet	40
	Planting trees in a filled organic pit	40
	Growing vegetables on Arborloo pits	42
	Making compost in small single shallow pits	43
4	*Fossa alterna* – The double pit compost toilet	45
	Managing the double pit compost toilet	45
	Examples of double pit composting toilets	46
	Building the double pit compost toilet	47
	Superstructures with rectangular slabs	51
5	Low-cost pedestals for simple pit toilets	55
	Very low-cost pedestal	55
	Low-cost pedestal with concrete seat	56
	Low-cost pedestal with plastic seat	57
6	Urine-diverting toilets	61
	How to build a single vault urine-diverting toilet	62
	Making the vault, step and lintel	63
	The urine-diverting pedestal	64
	Sequence of making a homemade urine-diverting pedestal with urine outlet pipe above slab level	64

	Making a simple urine-diverting platform	70
	Urine-diverting toilet installation details	71
	Urine-diverting superstructures	73
	Use and management of the urine-diverting toilet	74
	Processing the faeces	75
	Stages of building a twin pit composter for a single vault urine-diverting toilet	76
	Routine maintenance of the urine-diverting toilet	79
7	Upgrading the toilet system	81
	Upgrading using a round slab and ring beam	81
	Upgrading using a rectangular slab	83
8	Odour and fly control	85
	Odour control	85
	Fly control	86
9	A matter of hygiene and hand washing	89
	Simple hand washing devices	89
10	How to use toilet compost in the garden	93
	Testing crops in toilet pit compost	94
	Testing compost from a urine-diverting toilet	95
	Growing trees in toilet compost	96
11	How to use urine in the garden	99
	Crop trials using urine as a fertilizer	99
	Effect of urine use on maize growth on poor sandy soils: A field trial in Epworth near Harare	102
	Effect of urine treatment on trees	105
12	Summary	109
13	Conclusions	113
	Bibliography	115

Acknowledgements

From Zimbabwe I thank Christine Dean, Baidon Matambura, Marianne Knuth, Annie Kanyemba, Jim and Jill Latham, Ephraim Chimbunde, Edward Guzha, David Proudfoot, Frank Fleming and Ilona Howard. I am most grateful for the help, encouragement and collaboration with, colleagues in Malawi and Mozambique: Ned Breslin, Steven Sugden, Twitty Mukundia, Jim McGill, Gary Holm and Elias Chimulambe. I also wish to thank Obiero Ong'ang'a and Kinya Munyirwa from OSIENALA in Kenya. Many thanks are also due to Aussie Austin, Richard Holden, Dave Still and Stephen Nash from South Africa. Almaz Terrefe and Gunder Edstrom – thanks for the early enlightenment of ecosan. Thanks also to Piers Cross and Andreas Knapp of the WSP-AF programme, Nairobi. From Mexico I thank Ron Sawyer, George Anna Clark and Paco Arroyo who have offered much advice and encouragement. Uno Winblad is much thanked for his inspiration, long experience and much advice. Many thanks to Paul Calvert for his valuable insights and enormous encouragement from India. Many thanks indeed to Arno Rosemarin and staff of SEI, Stockholm for much encouragement and support. Many thanks also to Håkan Jönsson and Björn Vinnerås for important inputs and advice on urine use and the agricultural perspective. I offer sincere thanks and much gratitude to the late and much missed Steve Esrey from the USA. I wish to offer special thanks to a great friend and fellow traveller, Rolf Winberg. I am constantly indebted to Ingvar Andersson, for his long friendship, support and personal encouragement. I also offer thanks to Bengt Johansson and his staff at Sida for their encouragement and support which has made this work possible. Most importantly, I thank my wife Linda, for your patience, encouragement and every other possible support.

Peter Morgan

Figures

Figure 2.1	The simplest single pit compost toilet – the *Arborloo*	20
Figure 2.2	The double alternating pit compost toilet – the *Fossa alterna*	21
Figure 2.3	How the urine-diverting toilet works – side view	21
Figure 2.4	How the urine-diverting toilet works – front view	22
Figure 3.1	Simple compost toilet built on rectangular slab	23
Figure 3.2	Toilet house built over a round slab in Malawi	23
Figure 3.3	A healthy paw paw tree growing on a filled pit	24
Figure 3.4	Fruit trees can grow very well on these organic pits	24
Figure 3.5	Ring of bricks for the mould	25
Figure 3.6	Sheet of plastic laid in the mould	25
Figure 3.7	Measuring cement and river sand	26
Figure 3.8	Cement and reinforcing wires in mould	26
Figure 3.9	Mould after removal of squat hole insert	26
Figure 3.10	Forming the brick ring beam	26
Figure 3.11	Adding the second layer of bricks with anthill mortar	26
Figure 3.12	Completed brick ring beam	26
Figure 3.13	Brick mould on top of plastic sheet	27
Figure 3.14	Filling the spaces in the inner brick mould	28
Figure 3.15	Cement and wire reinforcement added to mould	28
Figure 3.16	Levelling off the concrete	28
Figure 3.17	Completed ring beam	28
Figure 3.18	Digging of hole inside ring beam	28
Figure 3.19	Dry leaves added to the pit	28
Figure 3.20	Toilet slab placed on ring beam	29
Figure 3.21	Trainees at Kufunda village	29
Figure 3.22	Circle of bricks 1.15m in diameter	31
Figure 3.23	Shaped bucket to make the squat hole	31
Figure 3.24	Mixing the cement and river sand	31
Figure 3.25	Adding the cement and sand mix to the mould	31
Figure 3.26	Wires added for reinforcement	31
Figure 3.27	Remainder of concrete mix added and levelled-off	31
Figure 3.28	Two brick circles for ring beam mould	32

Figure 3.29   Mixing the cement and river sand   33
Figure 3.30   Concrete mix added to mould   33
Figure 3.31   Wire reinforcement added   33
Figure 3.32   Remainder of concrete mix added and levelled-off   33
Figure 3.33   Digging the pit inside the brick ring beam   34
Figure 3.34   Packing soil around the brick ring beam   34
Figure 3.35   Placement of the concrete ring beam   34
Figure 3.36   Digging the pit inside the concrete ring beam   34
Figure 3.37   Using poles to build the toilet house   35
Figure 3.38   Toilet houses without a roof   35
Figure 3.39   Toilet house built with local materials   35
Figure 3.40   Interior of a toilet house   35
Figure 3.41   Laying down reinforcement wires   36
Figure 3.42   Levelling-off the concrete mix   36
Figure 3.43   Ring beam mould using bricks   36
Figure 3.44   Addition of wire for reinforcement   36
Figure 3.45   Moving the dry ring beam to a new site   37
Figure 3.46   Pit dug inside ring beam   37
Figure 3.47   Addition of leaves to pit   37
Figure 3.48   Anthill mortar packed around ring beam   37
Figure 3.49   Slab placed over ring beam   37
Figure 3.50   Gum poles, reeds and grass used to build the wall   37
Figure 3.51   Completed toilet house   38
Figure 3.52   Low-cost pedestal on top of slab   38
Figure 3.53   A simple structure made of poles and grass   39
Figure 3.54   A functional and attractive structure   39
Figure 3.55   An example of one simple style of structure   39
Figure 3.56   Another style of structure with a ventilation pipe   39
Figure 3.57   A portable structure built using a frame of poles   39
Figure 3.58   A portable structure built using a frame of steel   39
Figure 3.59   Mulberry cutting planted in a pot   41
Figure 3.60   Young mulberry tree   41
Figure 3.61   Banana tree growing on an *Arborloo* pit   41
Figure 3.62   Planting a mulberry tree on an *Arborloo* pit   41
Figure 3.63   A pumpkin crop in Ethiopia   42
Figure 3.64   Tomato plants growing on an *Arborloo* pit in Zvimba, Zimbabwe   42
Figure 3.65   Passion fruit growing on an *Arborloo* pit in Malawi   42

Figure 3.66	Pumpkin growing on a *Fossa alterna* pit in Zimbabwe	42
Figure 4.1	A portable structure using poles and reeds	46
Figure 4.2	A portable structure using a steel frame	46
Figure 4.3	A permanent structure housing both pits	46
Figure 4.4	Inside of the permanent structure	46
Figure 4.5	Measurements for the 1.2m X 0.9m concrete slab	47
Figure 4.6	A slab mould made with bricks and wood	48
Figure 4.7	The completed slab inside the mould	48
Figure 4.8	A slab mould made with bricks and wood	49
Figure 4.9	Ring beam mould using bricks	50
Figure 4.10	Digging the pit for the *Fossa alterna*	50
Figure 4.11	Adding leaves to the *Fossa alterna* pit	50
Figure 4.12	Completed *Fossa alterna* pit	50
Figure 4.13	Addition of the concrete slab	51
Figure 4.14	The completed pits for the double pit composting toilet	51
Figure 4.15	*Fossa alterna* using a wooden structure	52
Figure 4.16	*Fossa alterna* with grass walls	52
Figure 4.17	*Fossa alterna* at Woodhall Road, Harare	52
Figure 4.18	Inside a *Fossa alterna* that has been fitted with a pedestal	52
Figure 4.19	Fitting a portable superstructure to a *Fossa alterna* pit	53
Figure 4.20	A *Fossa alterna* after the second year	53
Figure 4.21	*Fossa alterna* with a permanent structure	53
Figure 4.22	Excavating the humus from the pit	53
Figure 4.23	Digging out compost in Hatcliffe, Zimbabwe	53
Figure 4.24	Digging out compost in Epworth, Zimbabwe	53
Figure 4.25	Construction of a portable structure for a *Fossa alterna*	54
Figure 4.26	A *Fossa alterna* with a permanent brick and thatch structure	54
Figure 4.27	*Fossa alterna* with a metal structure	54
Figure 4.28	Brick double pit composting toilet	54
Figure 5.1	Construction of the very low-cost pedestal	55
Figure 5.2	Painted very low-cost pedestal	55
Figure 5.3	Adding concrete to the toilet seat mould	57
Figure 5.4	Building up the sides of the bucket	57
Figure 5.5	Painting the concrete pedestal	57
Figure 5.6	Finished concrete pedestal	57
Figure 5.7	Ring of wire added to plastic toilet seat	58
Figure 5.8	Plastic toilet seat filled with strong concrete	58

Figure 5.9	Plastic bucket placed over toilet seat	58
Figure 5.10	Concrete reinforcement added around first layer of concrete	58
Figure 5.11	Completed pedestal placed in wooden mould	59
Figure 5.12	Completed low-cost pedestal with plastic seat	59
Figure 6.1	The brick mould for the base slab	62
Figure 6.2	The brick mould for the toilet slab	62
Figure 6.3	Building the vault using bricks on their edge	63
Figure 6.4	Testing the height of the vault access	63
Figure 6.5	Fitting the vault access slab	64
Figure 6.6	Front view of the vault with the toilet slab placed on top	64
Figure 6.7	Materials for the homemade urine-diverting toilet pedestal	65
Figure 6.8	Cutting the base off the bucket	65
Figure 6.9	Marking the plastic base	65
Figure 6.10	The cut plastic base	65
Figure 6.11	The cut base fitted half-way up the bucket at an angle	67
Figure 6.12	Attaching the cut base with wire	67
Figure 6.13	Fitting of the pipe bend to the bucket	67
Figure 6.14	Inside view of the fitted pipe bend	67
Figure 6.15	Using a hot wire to make a hole through the plastic toilet seat ribs	67
Figure 6.16	The toilet seat with a threaded loop of wire	67
Figure 6.17	Concrete added to the toilet seat	68
Figure 6.18	Bucket placed onto the toilet seat	68
Figure 6.19	Bent wire added around the bucket	68
Figure 6.20	Concrete added half-way up the bucket	68
Figure 6.21	Upper-half of bucket covered in concrete	68
Figure 6.22	Bucket and seat turned over and placed into base mould	68
Figure 6.23	Wire added for reinforcement	69
Figure 6.24	Completed pedestal curing	69
Figure 6.25	Sealing the urine diverter against the bucket wall	69
Figure 6.26	Sealing the top side of the urine diverter	69
Figure 6.27	Urine outlet pipe attached	69
Figure 6.28	Outlet pipe led to the back of the toilet	69
Figure 6.29	Painting the pedestal	70
Figure 6.30	Close-up of the base of the pedestal	70
Figure 6.31	Urine-diverting pedestal installed	70

Figure 6.32	Exterior of toilet house with urine-diverting toilet	70
Figure 6.33	Top-view of a urine-diverting squat toilet	71
Figure 6.34	Side-view of a urine-diverting squat toilet	71
Figure 6.35	Urine-diverting pedestal with a handsome wooden seat	71
Figure 6.36	Top-view of the a urine-diverting pedestal	71
Figure 6.37	The brick mould for the base slab	72
Figure 6.38	The brick mould for the toilet slab	72
Figure 6.39	Side-vault for urine collection	73
Figure 6.40	Internal view of vault with plastic bucket placed for collection of faeces	73
Figure 6.41	Superstructure made of polyethylene pipes covered with a plastic cloth	74
Figure 6.42	A brick single-vault urine-diverting toilet	74
Figure 6.43	Removal of bucket of faeces	75
Figure 6.44	Emptying the bucket of faeces into the secondary composting site	75
Figure 6.45	Emptying faeces into a small shallow pit	76
Figure 6.46	Cement jars for composting faeces	76
Figure 6.47	Casting ring beams	77
Figure 6.48	Cured ring beams	77
Figure 6.49	Dug-out pits	77
Figure 6.50	Twin pits ready for use with right-side pit filled with leaves	77
Figure 6.51	Wooden lid for active composting pit	78
Figure 6.52	Bucket of faeces ready for emptying	78
Figure 6.53	Emptying the bucket of faeces into the pit	78
Figure 6.54	Active composting pit covered by wooden lid	78
Figure 6.55	Spider webs inside the vault	79
Figure 6.56	Spider webs and spiders inside the vault	79
Figure 6.57	Cleaned urine-diverting toilet	80
Figure 6.58	Wild basil Ocimum canum, a mosquito repellent	80
Figure 7.1	Urine-diverting pedestal fitted to a Fossa alterna system	82
Figure 7.2	Urine off-take fitted above the base of the pedestal	82
Figure 7.3	Ring beam laid on level ground	82
Figure 7.4	Brick wall built-up on ring beam	82
Figure 7.5	Slab and pedestal fitted on built-up base	82
Figure 7.6	Concrete vault access door	82
Figure 7.7	Structure around upgraded toilet	83

Figure 7.8	Urine-diverting pipe attached to base of pedestal	83
Figure 7.9	*Arborloo* built on a rectangular slab	83
Figure 7.10	*Fossa alterna* built on a rectangular slab	83
Figure 7.11	*Fossa alterna* upgraded with a non urine-diverting pedestal	84
Figure 7.12	*Fossa alterna* upgraded with a urine-diverting pedestal	84
Figure 7.13	Urine-diverting pedestal mounted above the ground	84
Figure 7.14	Urine pipe located below the slab	84
Figure 8.1	The effect of a vent pipe	86
Figure 8.2	Urine-diverting pedestal	86
Figure 8.3	Addition of wood ash to the pit to control fly breeding	87
Figure 9.1	A simple plastic cup hand washing device	90
Figure 9.2	Used water falls on to plants below	90
Figure 9.3	A simple tin can hand washing device	90
Figure 9.4	Using the tin can hand washing device	90
Figure 9.5	Adding water to the tin can	91
Figure 9.6	Tin can with a single hole	91
Figure 9.7	Tin can and a bar of soap	91
Figure 9.8	Piercing a hole in the plastic bottle	91
Figure 9.9	Putting-on the screw cap	91
Figure 9.10	Open screw cap for hand washing	91
Figure 10.1	Sandy toilet compost	93
Figure 10.2	Humus-like toilet compost	93
Figure 10.3	Toilet compost dug out of a *Fossa alterna* pit	94
Figure 10.4	Inspecting the toilet compost	94
Figure 10.5	Spinach growth test - the bucket on the right has soil enhanced with toilet compost	94
Figure 10.6	Covo growth test – the bucket on the right has soil enhanced with toilet compost	94
Figure 10.7	Lettuce growth test - the bucket on the right has soil enhanced with toilet compost	95
Figure 10.8	Onion growth test - the harvest on the right was grown in soil enhanced with toilet compost	95
Figure 10.9	Tomato seedlings	95
Figure 10.10	Young tomato plants	95
Figure 10.11	Tomato plants growing	96
Figure 10.12	Crop of young tomatoes	96
Figure 10.13	Digging the pit for the tree	97
Figure 10.14	Digging-out the toilet compost	97

Figure 10.15	Tree pit filled with toilet compost	97
Figure 10.16	Bricks laid around the tree pit	97
Figure 10.17	Planting a young mulberry tree	97
Figure 10.18	The mulberry tree after four months of growth	97
Figure 11.1	Rape crop trials	99
Figure 11.2	Rape crop yields	99
Figure 11.3	Spinach crop trials	100
Figure 11.4	Spinach crop yields	100
Figure 11.5	Mint after urine treatment	100
Figure 11.6	Passion fruit after urine treatment	100
Figure 11.7	A prize specimen of onion	101
Figure 11.8	Maize fed with water only and diluted urine	102
Figure 11.9	Maize cob yields	102
Figure 11.10	Measuring urine	103
Figure 11.11	Maize seeds planted on 11 November 2004	103
Figure 11.12	Application of urine to a young maize plant	103
Figure 11.13	Comparison between urine-treated and untreated maize crops	103
Figure 11.14	Digging a hole for urine application	104
Figure 11.15	Applying the urine	104
Figure 11.16	First sign of tassel from 17 January 2005	104
Figure 11.17	First sign of the cob from 17 January 2005	104
Figure 11.18	Maize crop on 31 January 2005 – comparison of urine-treated maize with untreated maize	105
Figure 11.19	Urine applied to a banana tree directly from the toilet	106
Figure 11.20	Urine applied to a banana tree through a bucket	106
Figure 11.21	Preparation for urine application in a hole near the tree	106
Figure 11.22	Application of the urine into the hole	106
Figure 11.23	Bucket fitted with small pipe to apply urine	107
Figure 11.24	Inside view of bucket with pipe to apply urine	107
Figure 13.1	Eco-toilet in Ruwa, Zimbabwe	113

CHAPTER 1
Introduction

Most of the rural population of Africa do not have access to safe and reliable toilets. A good toilet, together with a safe reliable water supply and the practice of good personal hygiene can do much to improve personal and family health and wellbeing. There is an urgent need for the construction of simple, low-cost, affordable toilets that are easy to build and maintain and are relatively free of odours and flies.

This book describes how to make a range of toilets that also make compost. The compost is useful in the vegetable garden and can also be used for growing trees. The simplest are low-cost pit toilets and a builder is not required once the householder has learned the basic methods of construction. The more complex toilets use a method known as urine diversion and a builder will be required to construct this type.

Fly and odour problems can be reduced by regularly adding soil, wood ash and leaves to the excreta in the pit. Fly problems are worst during the warm wet season. If ash and leaves are not available, soil alone helps. But adding ash and leaves helps make better compost. The more soil is added the better, but this must be offset against filling the pit too fast. These extra ingredients also help turn the mix into compost more efficiently. It is possible to grow a tree directly in the filled toilet pit if it is planted in a layer of soil placed above the compost. It is also possible to dig out the compost after a suitable time and use this to fertilize the vegetable garden or plant trees. So the simple toilet can have many valuable uses, in addition to being a safe way to dispose of excreta.

Over the years it is possible to improve on the original simple toilet using the same concrete slab. It is a small amount to pay for something that gives so much benefit to the family.

CHAPTER 2
Compost-making toilets

Three types of compost-making toilets will be described in this book. Two are shallow pit toilets and the third is a urine-diverting toilet.

- The first uses a single shallow pit, about 1.0m deep.
- The next uses two shallow pits, about 1.5m deep, which are used alternately.
- The third is built on a vault above the ground and uses a urine-diverting principle where the urine and faeces are separated.

Each toilet is built with a concrete slab. This can be made round or rectangular in shape, using cement and clean sharp river sand and 3mm wire. Slabs are easy to make once the method is known. The final strength depends on the curing process, which means keeping the concrete wet, once it has set hard, for at least 7–10 days after it has been made. Portland cement (PC15) must be used to make concrete, not plaster cement. The cement should be as fresh as possible. Good cement and sand and good mixing and curing are important.

The shape of the slab, round or rectangular, may depend on the type of house structure built for privacy. Square box-like houses fit best over the rectangular slab. Round traditional houses fit best over the round slab. If the slab is mounted over a shallow pit, the pit should be protected with a ring of bricks or circle of concrete called a ring beam. If the soil is very unstable then it should be lined with bricks. If the soil is so unstable that it must be lined with bricks, it is best to make two pits and dig out the compost for use elsewhere. In the urine-diverting toilet a brick chamber or vault is built up above ground level on a concrete base. The concrete slab is mounted on the vault and a urine-diverting pedestal is then mounted on the slab and a house for privacy built on top.

Arborloo – The simplest single pit compost toilet

In this concept the pit is shallow, about 1.0 to 1.5m deep, and the toilet site is temporary (Figure 2.1). Excreta, soil, ash and leaves are added to the pit. The toilet – consisting of a ring beam, slab and structure – moves from one site to the next at 6 to 12-month intervals. The old site is covered with soil and left to compost. A tree is planted on the old site, preferably during the rains.

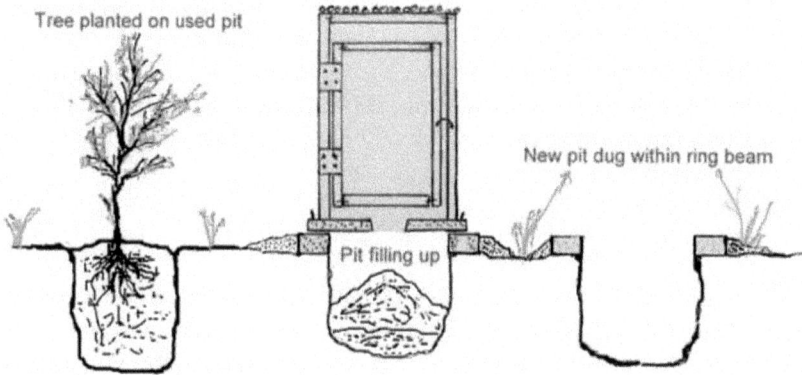

Figure 2.1   The simplest single pit compost toilet – the *Arborloo*

Fossa alterna – The double alternating pit compost toilet

In this concept there are two permanently sited shallow pits, about 1.5m deep and dug close to each other, which are used alternately (Figure 2.2). For a medium sized family the pit takes about 12 months to fill up and this same period allows sufficient time for the mix of excreta, soil, ash and leaves to form compost which can be excavated. Every year one pit is excavated whilst the other becomes full. If the pits remain stable this process can continue for years.

The urine-diverting toilet uses a special pedestal or squat plate which separates the urine from the faeces (Figure 2.3 and Figure 2.4). In this case, the faeces fall into a 20 litre bucket held in a brick vault. Soil and ash are added to the bucket after every deposit is made. The contents of the bucket are removed regularly and placed in another site (secondary compost site) to make compost. This process takes between 6–12 months. The urine collects in a plastic container. Both toilet compost and urine add fertility to the soil and can enhance food production.

COMPOST-MAKING TOILETS   21

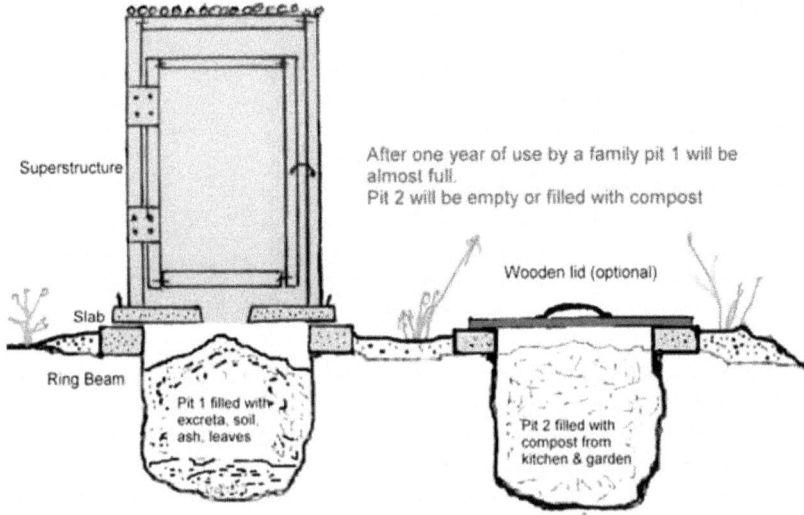

Figure 2.2   The double alternating pit compost toilet – the *Fossa alterna*

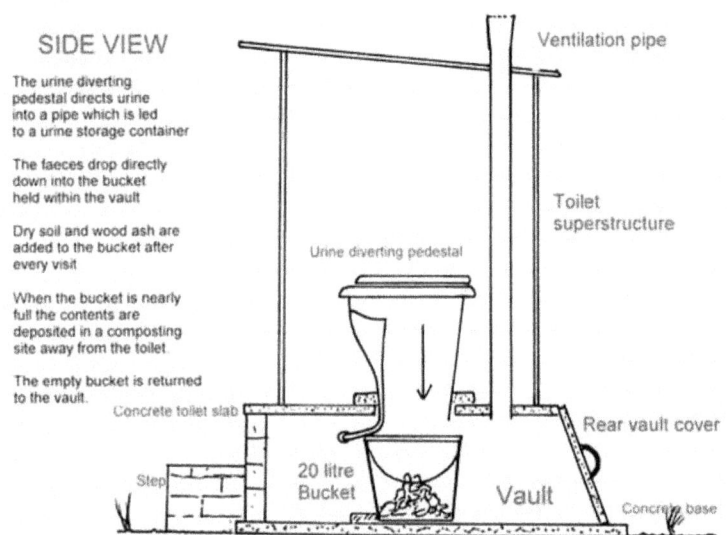

Figure 2.3   How the urine-diverting toilet works – side view

22 TOILETS THAT MAKE COMPOST

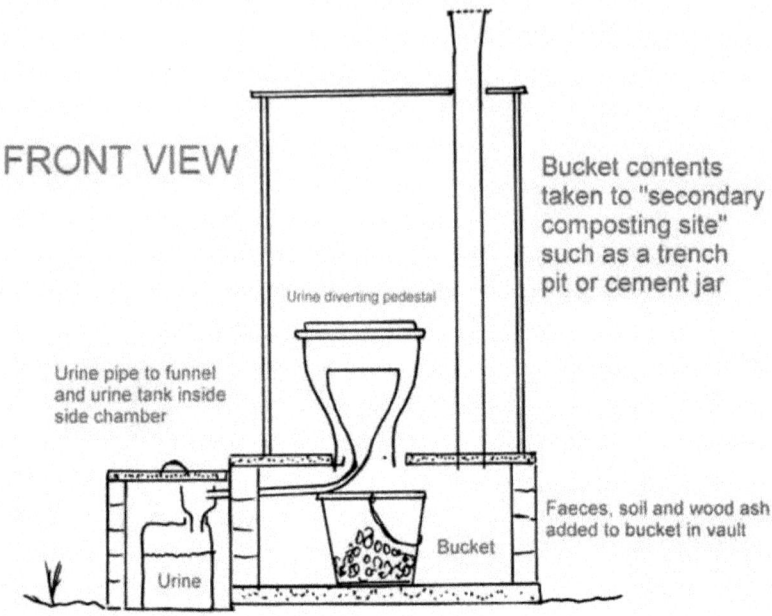

Figure 2.4 How the urine-diverting toilet works – front view

CHAPTER 3
Arborloo – The single pit compost toilet

The single pit compost toilet, or *Arborloo* (Figure 3.1 and Figure 3.2), is a simple toilet is made up of 4 parts:

- The pit
- The ring beam to protect the pit
- The concrete slab which sits on the ring beam
- The toilet house which provides privacy.

The pit fills up with a mix of excreta, soil, wood ash and leaves. Leaves are put in the base of the pit before use and every day some soil and wood ash are added to the pit. Dry leaves are also added to the pit from time to time, if available. No garbage is put down the pit. Garbage such as plastic, rags, bottles, and tin cans are placed in a separate garbage pit dug for this purpose.

Figure 3.1 Simple compost toilet built on rectangular slab

Figure 3.2 Toilet house built over a round slab in Malawi

24 TOILETS THAT MAKE COMPOST

When soil, ash and leaves are regularly added to excreta, the conversion into compost takes place at a faster rate compared to excreta to which nothing has been added. The daily addition of soil and ash also helps to reduce flies and smells. If ash or leaves are not available add soil alone – it helps!

When the *Arborloo* pit is full, the parts of the toilet are moved to another place, rebuilt and used in the same way again. A thick layer of soil is placed over the filled pit. A young tree is planted in this soil and is watered and cared for. It is often best to allow the pit contents to compost for a while, top up with soil again and then plant the young tree at the start of the rainy season.

After some years a large mature tree will be growing where the toilet was before (Figure 3.3 and Figure 3.4). A new orchard of fruit trees or a woodlot of gum trees will be growing, using nutrients derived from the compost formed from excreta. In fact most trees will grow on an *Arborloo* pit if well cared for, including ornamental, shade and indigenous trees. Urine diluted with water (1:5) can help many trees grow faster, including banana, mango and mulberry trees. By using this simple principle, the nutrients in our excreta can be recycled into something valuable – without any handling of the compost. Trees are good to look at, and they can provide food, shade, fuel and building materials and also consolidate the soil. They improve the environment and our world enormously.

Figure 3.3 A healthy paw paw tree growing on a filled pit

Figure 3.4 Fruit trees can grow very well on these organic pits

Figure 3.5 Ring of bricks for the mould   **Figure 3.6** Sheet of plastic laid in the mould

How to build the single pit compost toilet

The first step is to make a small concrete slab. The round slab has a 1m diameter for a 0.8m diameter pit. The concrete slab is made with a mixture of Portland cement (PC 15 for concrete work – masonry cement should NOT be used) and good quality river sand (sharp feel and clean) with some wire reinforcing. The mould for the concrete slab is made from a ring of bricks (Figure 3.5) or tin loop laid out on level ground. The bricks are laid around a circle marked on the ground, one metre in diameter. A plastic sheet is placed over the brick mould and the squat hole is made by placing a shaped plastic bucket or shaped bricks in the slab mould (Figure 3.6).

A concrete mixture is required to make the slab. The concrete mix for a one metre diameter slab is 8 litres of cement (PC 15) and 30 litres river sand (Figure 3.7). A 50kg bag of cement contains about 40 litres cement, enough for 5 slabs. If there is doubt about the quality of the cement use 10 litres of cement and 30 litres of clean river sand. The sand and cement must be very well mixed on the ground or in a wheel barrow. After mixing the dry sand and cement add about 2–3 litres of water to make a stiff mix like porridge. Mix thoroughly again.

Add half the mix to the slab mould and spread out evenly. Add 4 reinforcing wires each 3mm to 4mm in diameter and 90cm long in a square shape around the squat hole (Figure 3.8). Strong barbed wire will do. Then add the rest of the concrete mixture. Spread out evenly. Also, ram down hard with a wooden float. Smooth off with a steel trowel. Add two thick wire handles on either side for lifting if required. After 3 hours take out the bricks or bucket from the squat hole and make the edges neat with a trowel (Figure 3.9). Cover the slab with a plastic sheet overnight. The following morning – wet down the slab and cover again. The slab must be covered and kept wet for at least 7 days and preferably 10–14 days to cure properly before moving.

26 TOILETS THAT MAKE COMPOST

Figure 3.7 Measuring cement and river sand

Figure 3.8 Cement and reinforcing wires in mould

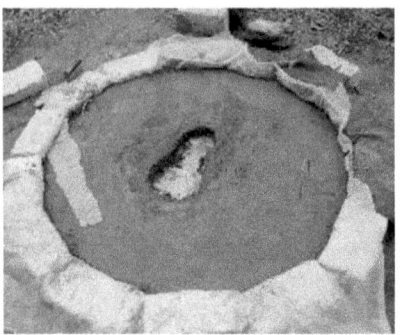

Figure 3.9 Mould after removal of squat hole insert

Figure 3.10 Forming the brick ring beam

Figure 3.11 Adding the second layer of bricks with anthill mortar

Figure 3.12 Completed brick ring beam

How to make ring beams

The ring beam is a ring of bricks or concrete which is placed at the top of the pit. The concrete slab is laid on the ring beam. The ring beam helps to keep the top of the pit from falling in. It also supports the concrete slab, which is raised above the ground level. The ring beam also diverts rainwater away from the toilet site. The pit is dug down inside the ring beam once it has been laid. The soil taken from the pit is rammed in place around the ring beam to make the toilet safer and raise the ground level around the toilet. The ring beam can be made of bricks and anthill mortar or it can be made from wire reinforced concrete using a mix of cement and clean river sand. It is important to raise the toilet base above ground level to avoid flooding during the rainy season. The ring beam is made on slightly raised ground where the toilet is to be built.

To make the smaller brick ring beam with an internal diameter of 80cm, get some fired farm bricks and mark a circle on the ground 80cm in diameter. Lay the bricks around the circle (Figure 3.10). Make up some anthill mortar (*Ivhu re pa churi*) by breaking up anthill soil and mixing with water. Using a trowel add the anthill mortar between and above the bricks. Then add a second layer of bricks on the first layer (Figure 3.11). The upper layer of bricks should sit on the joint between bricks of the first course. Use the anthill mortar to hold all the bricks together (Figure 3.12).

If bricks are not available, or if extra cement is available, use clean river sand and fresh cement to make a concrete ring beam which will last for many years. The same mixture for making the concrete slab is used to make the concrete ring beam: 8 litres of cement and 30 litres of river sand. But the cement must be fresh and the river sand very clean. The measurements and the mixes must be exact and 7–10 days curing for the cement is required. If the cement is not fresh or the river sand is not clean it is best to make a stronger mix of 10 litres of cement and 30 litres of river sand.

Figure 3.13 Brick mould on top of plastic sheet

28 TOILETS THAT MAKE COMPOST

Figure 3.14 Filling the spaces in the inner brick mould

Figure 3.15 Cement and wire reinforcement added to mould

Figure 3.16 Levelling off the concrete

Figure 3.17 Completed ring beam

Figure 3.18 Digging of hole inside ring beam

Figure 3.19 Dry leaves added to the pit

ARBORLOO – THE SINGLE PIT COMPOST TOILET

Level off some ground and lay a plastic sheet over the ground. Take some bricks and make two circles of bricks. The concrete ring beam will be made in between the two circles of bricks. Lay the bricks so the outer and inner circles will make a ring beam in between them, which is 85cm inside and 115cm outside. Thus the width of the ring beam is 15cm all round. Fill the spaces opened up between inner bricks with wet sand (Figure 3.13 and Figure 3.14).

Once the brick mould has been made, make up the concrete mixture of 8 litres fresh cement with 30 litres good river sand. Mix the dry parts thoroughly first then mix with about 3 litres of fresh water. Mix thoroughly again. Add half of this mixture to the mould and level off. Then take a length of 3mm wire and place above the concrete mix all around the beam about half way between the inner and outer bricks (Figure 3-15). A second ring of wire adds extra strength. Then add the remainder of the concrete mix to the mould and level off with a wooden float (Figure 3-16).

Cover with a plastic sheet and leave overnight. The following morning, wet the ring beam and keep wet and covered for 7–10 days to cure. Every day the concrete gets stronger. After 7–10 days the ring beam can be lifted and put into place at the toilet site on levelled ground (Figure 3.17). Dig down a hole within the ring beam to at least 1.0m and up to 1.5m below surface depending on soil type (Figure 3.18). Place soil around ring beam and ram in place hard.

A big sack of dry leaves is added to the pit (Figure 3.19). These help the contents of the pit to compost. After adding the leaves the slab is moved on to the ring beam (Figure 3.20). It is best to lay the slab in some mortar placed on the ring beam. This can be made of anthill mortar or weak cement and sand (20:1). This packing allows the slab to rest evenly on the ring beam and also forms a seal. Figure 3.21 shows a group of trainees at Kufunda village (Ruwa, Zimbabwe) being taught how to build a simple compost toilet.

Figure 3.20 Toilet slab placed on ring beam   **Figure 3.21** Trainees at Kufunda village

The ring beam method is suitable for most soils which are moderately firm. It also works in sandy soils which have some firmness. But the method is not suitable for very loose sandy soils which collapse easily. In this case some sort of pit lining will be necessary. If bricks or blocks are used to line the pit, it is best to use the toilet system to make compost which can later be dug out rather than plant a tree directly in the pit. The excavated pit can be used again. To use bricks or blocks to line a temporary pit is uneconomical. The excavated compost can also be used for tree growing as well as vegetable growing. When used for growing new trees, a tree pit 60cm x 60cm and 60cm deep can be dug and the toilet compost added to this. The tree is best planted in a layer of soil placed above the pit compost. The pit composting process takes up to a year in a shallow pit if plenty of soil, ash and leaves have been added. It may take several years if no extra ingredients are added. Pit compost can be transferred to a tree pit relatively safely after 6 months of composting, since it is covered with topsoil. Young trees are best planted during the rainy season.

By making the slab slightly larger (1.15m) it can be fitted over a concrete ring beam with an internal diameter of 1m. This relatively small increase in pit diameter from 0.8m to 1m increases the pit volume by 1.5 times, and thus extends the pit life by about that amount. Even larger slabs and ring beams can be used. These use more cement and are heavier to lift but extra pit volume is gained.

A 1.15m diameter concrete slab can be made with 10 litres of fresh cement mixed with 50 litres of clean river sand with at least four 3mm wires used as reinforcing. This slab is fitted over a concrete ring beam with an internal diameter of 1m and an external diameter of 1.4m (ring beam width 20cm). This ring beam also uses 10 litres of cement and 50 litres of sand. So the slab and the concrete ring beam each use 10 litres of cement (total 20 litres) which is half a 50kg bag of cement. The pit is dug down inside the ring beam down to a depth of between 1 and 2 metres. Soil from the pit is heaped around the ring beam and rammed in place. A suitable house is built around and over the slab for privacy. Ideally it should be fitted with a roof. Flies and odours can be reduced by regularly adding soil, ash and leaves to the pit to cover fresh excreta added. But in the hot wet summer months it may be impossible to control them completely.

This slab and ring beam combination can also be used to build a normal shallow pit toilet with a maximum depth of around 2 metres if the soil is firm enough. Where ring beams are used the house must be made of light materials like poles and grass. The brick built superstructure is too heavy for the ring beam method. Even with the normal pit toilet, steps must be taken to reduce flies and odours and the addition of soil, ash and leaves is recommended. It also helps to keep the inside of the toilet very clean, and a cover can be placed over the hole when the latrine is not in use. Eventually

ARBORLOO – THE SINGLE PIT COMPOST TOILET   31

Figure 3.22 Circle of bricks 1.15m in diameter

Figure 3.23 Shaped bucket to make the squat hole

Figure 3.24 Mixing the cement and river sand

Figure 3.25 Adding the cement and sand mix to the mould

Figure 3.26 Wires added for reinforcement

Figure 3.27 Remainder of concrete mix added and levelled-off

excreta added to a pit will compost even if little soil is added, but this may take 5–10 years depending on the conditions. Composting takes place faster in unlined pits with an earth wall and greater drainage area compared to pits lined with bricks. Rubbish like plastic and rags should not be added to the pit but placed in a separate garbage pit.

To make the 1.15m concrete slab, lay a plastic sheet on level ground and lay bricks in a circle, 1.15m in diameter to make a mould (Figure 3.22). Add a shaped bucket or bricks to make the squat hole (Figure 3.23). Make a mix of 10 litres Portland cement and 50 litres clean river sand (Figure 3.24). Add about half of the mix to the brick mould and level off (Figure 3.25).

Steel wires 3mm in diameter are used for reinforcing. For the larger slab at least four pieces are laid in a square around the squat hole (Figure 3.26). Eight pieces would be better. After laying down the wires, add the rest of the concrete mix and level off (Figure 3.27). The slab is left to cure for at least 7 days and preferably 14 days, being kept wet at all times after the hardening process. Once cured, the slab can be moved to the toilet site. The ring beam is laid down first on levelled ground, the pit dug and the slab added.

Figure 3.28 Two brick circles for ring beam mould

To make a concrete ring beam with a 1m internal diameter, lay plastic sheet on ground and make two circles of bricks (Figure 3.28). The concrete for the ring beam is laid between the two circles. The inner diameter should be 1.0 metre and the outer 1.4 metres. This makes the width of the ring beam 20cm. Pre-cut sticks can be used to make the measurement. Make up a mix of 10 litres cement and 50 litres clean river sand and mix into concrete (Figure 3.29). Add half the mix to the brick mould and level off (Figure 3.30).

Add two complete circles of 3mm wire on the concrete (Figure 3.31). Then add the remainder of the concrete mix and level off with wooden float

ARBORLOO – THE SINGLE PIT COMPOST TOILET 33

Figure 3.29 Mixing the cement and river sand

Figure 3.30 Concrete mix added to mould

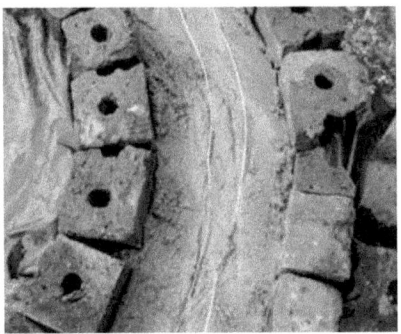

Figure 3.31 Wire reinforcement added

Figure 3.32 Remainder of concrete mix added and levelled-off

(Figure 3.32). Cure in the same way as concrete slab. When slab and ring beam have cured, move both on to toilet site. Place the ring beam on levelled ground and dig pit. Heap and ram soil around ring beam. Place slab on ring beam on bed of weak mortar.

For the brick ring beam, the pit is dug down inside the ring beam (Figure 3.33), and the extracted soil being placed around the ring beam and rammed hard in place (Figure 3.34). The pit is dug down at least 1 one metre and up to 1.5 metres deep. The deeper the pit the longer it will last.

For the concrete ring beam, it is important to make the ring beam first and place it in position at the toilet site before digging the pit (Figure 3.35). The pit is dug inside the ring beam. Soil taken from the pit is placed around the ring beam and rammed hard in place (Figure 3.36). This raises the soil level around the toilet site and helps protect the pit from erosion caused by rainfall.

34 TOILETS THAT MAKE COMPOST

Figure 3.33 Digging the pit inside the brick ring beam

Figure 3.34 Packing soil around the brick ring beam

Figure 3.35 Placement of the concrete ring beam

Figure 3.36 Digging the pit inside the concrete ring beam

Building the toilet house (superstructure)

The toilet house is built around the ring beam and slab with local materials like poles and grass (Figure 3.37). Where a ring beam is used the structure should be light. The use of poles and grass is a traditional method, sometimes without a roof (Figure 3.38). A roofed structure is better (Figure 3.39), and it is good to have a neat interior with soil and ash ready (Figure 3.40).

Superstructures are used to add privacy to the toilet. There are many ways of making the superstructure from simple low-cost materials. It is best to make a roof to fit over the structure for shade and to keep the rain out. This also helps control flies. *Arborloo* structures should be made in such a way that they can be moved easily or dismantled easily for movement from one location to the next. The structures are generally light and made of traditional materials.

ARBORLOO – THE SINGLE PIT COMPOST TOILET 35

Figure 3.37 Using poles to build the toilet house

Figure 3.38 Toilet houses without a roof

Figure 3.39 Toilet house built with local materials

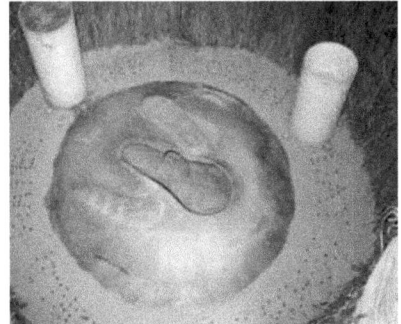

Figure 3.40 Interior of a toilet house

Making an *Arborloo* fitted with a pedestal

This series of photos shows a 1m diameter slab being made for use with a concrete ring beam and homemade pedestal. Several types of homemade pedestal can be used (see Chapter 5). To cast the slab, mark out a 1m diameter ring on flat ground. Surround with bricks and lay down plastic sheet inside. Insert mould for making the hole 30mm to rear of slab. Cut suitable lengths of 3mm wire. Make mix of cement (10 litres) and clean river sand (30 litres). Add half the mix first and then add the wires (Figure 3.41). Add rest of the mix and level off (Figure 3.42). Cover with plastic sheet and leave to cure for 7 days. Keep wet after the concrete has set.

Make the ring beam by laying bricks so the inner diameter is 85cm and the outer diameter 115cm (Figure 3.43). Fill openings between inner bricks with wet sand. The concrete mix is the same as for the slab. Add half the concrete

36 TOILETS THAT MAKE COMPOST

Figure 3.41 Laying down reinforcement wires

Figure 3.42 Levelling-off the concrete mix

Figure 3.43 Ring beam mould using bricks

Figure 3.44 Addition of wire for reinforcement

mix and then add at least 2 rings of 3mm wire in a loop (Figure 3.44). Add the remainder of the concrete and level off. Allow to cure for several days.

Keep ring beam in original site or roll to new site (Figure 3.45). Loosen earth and bed down ring beam in topsoil. Dig down within the ring beam one metre deep – max 1.5m (Figure 3.46). Add a sack full of leaves to the inside base of the pit (Figure 3.47). Make up mix of anthill mortar by adding water to broken anthill soil. Place mortar on top of ring beam and bed in the slab into the mortar (Figure 3.48).

After placing slab in position over the ring beam (Figure 3.49) make the superstructure. This can be as simple as using treated gum poles for uprights with reeds and grass used as walls (Figure 3.50). The reeds and grass can be made up as panels. Later refinements including a roof can be added (Figure 3.51).

ARBORLOO – THE SINGLE PIT COMPOST TOILET

Figure 3.45 Moving the dry ring beam to a new site

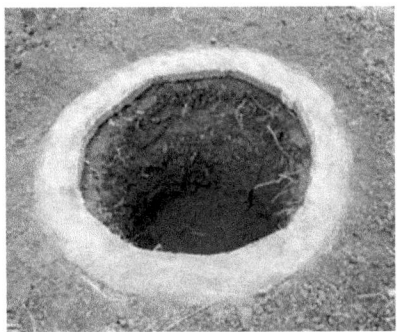

Figure 3.46 Pit dug inside ring beam

Figure 3.47 Addition of leaves to pit

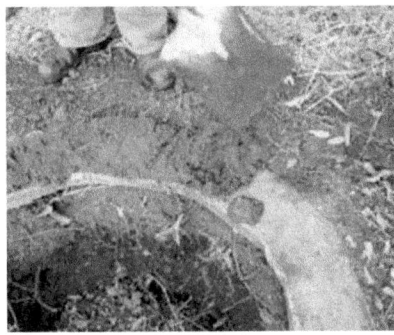

Figure 3.48 Anthill mortar packed around ring beam

Figure 3.49 Slab placed over ring beam

Figure 3.50 Gum poles, reeds and grass used to build the wall

38 TOILETS THAT MAKE COMPOST

Figure 3.51 Completed toilet house

Figure 3.52 Low-cost pedestal on top of slab

The low-cost pedestal is added on top of the slab (Figure 3.52). This one uses only concrete and an insert of a 10 litre bucket (see Chapter 5). A hand washing device should also be made and hung inside the toilet (see Chapter 9). A sack or bucket of dry soil and wood ash should be provided inside. Soil and wood ash can be combined (3:1). Add a small cupful after each use. Adding dry leaves also helps the composting process in the pit. The added soil and ash also assists composting and reduces flies and odours.

When the pit is nearly full, move ring beam, slab and structure to another site and top up the pit with soil. Wait until the rains before planting a suitable tree. Protect tree from animals and keep watered. Most trees (fruit, indigenous, fuel and timber) will grow well.

Types of superstructure

Most simple structures are built with poles and grass (Figure 3.53). Even these simple building materials can be used to make a functional and attractive structure (Figure 3.54). A huge range of home built structures can be made with simple building materials (Figure 3.55), including those fitted with homemade ventilation pipes (Figure 3.56).

Portable structures can be built over a frame of poles (Figure 3.57) or steel (Figure 3.58). Grass, reeds or plastic bags and other materials can be used for walling. The roof can be made of thin corrugated iron or even plastic sheet laid over chicken wire mounted on a frame and covered with grass.

ARBORLOO – THE SINGLE PIT COMPOST TOILET

Figure 3.53 A simple structure made of poles and grass

Figure 3.54 A functional and attractive structure

Figure 3.55 An example of one simple style of structure

Figure 3.56 Another style of structure with a ventilation pipe

Figure 3.57 A portable structure built using a frame of poles

Figure 3.58 A portable structure built using a frame of steel

How to use the single pit compost toilet

When using a compost toilet regularly add dry soil, wood ash and leaves to the pit as well as excreta. This mix of excreta, soil, ash and leaves helps to make good compost in the pit. Add soil and ash after every visit to deposit faeces, about a small cup full of soil and some ash, but not after every visit to add urine. Sometimes add extra leaves from time to time. If ash and leaves are not available the addition of soil alone helps.

It is important to keep the toilet clean. Never put any kind of rubbish or garbage down the pit like such as plastic and rags. Use the toilet until the pit is nearly full. Keep fly breeding under control by adding plenty of soil and ash if possible. When the pit is nearly full it is time to move the single pit compost toilet to a new location.

Remove the superstructure or take it apart. Remove the concrete slab and ring beam. If it is a brick ring beam, take the bricks apart and re-use them in the new site. Cover the contents of the pit with a thick layer (15cm deep) of good soil. Now rebuild the brick ring beam in a new site. If a concrete ring beam is used it just needs to be moved to the new site. Dig a new pit inside the ring beam and surround the ring beam with soil and ram hard. Add a sack of leaves to the bottom of the pit. Place the slab on the new ring beam and rebuild or refit the superstructure. Then start to use the new toilet.

Planting trees in a filled organic pit

There are three main ways to use a filled pit. The first is to cover the pit contents with plenty of good soil at least 15cm deep. Leave this pit to settle. Add more soil and wait for the rains before planting a new young tree. The second way is to cover the pit contents with plenty of good soil at least 15cm deep and plant a young tree immediately in the added soil and look after it. It will require protection from animals and frequent watering. The third method is to allow the pit contents to turn into compost and dig the compost out later, after 6–12 months, for use on the garden or for trees.

Mulberries are tasty fruit and are easy to grow. They can be grown from cuttings (Figure 3.59). Place a cutting in a pot or bucket and fill it with good fertile soil. Keep it watered and protected. It will then grow larger and stronger in preparation for planting on top of the *Arborloo* pit in 6–12 months time (Figure 3.60). Once planted, adding wood ash provides potassium which helps fruiting. Adding compost and leaf mulch also helps.

Most trees grow well on *Arborloo* pits. Good fruit trees for *Arborloo* pits are mulberry, avocado, guava, mango, paw paw and banana. Figure 3.61 shows the luxuriant growth of a banana on an *Arborloo* pit in Malawi. Figure 3.62 shows the first trainees at Kufunda Village Training Centre in Ruwa, Zimbabwe, planting a mulberry tree on an *Arborloo* pit. Many other types of tree including

ARBORLOO – THE SINGLE PIT COMPOST TOILET

Figure 3.59 Mulberry cutting planted in a pot

Figure 3.60 Young mulberry tree

Figure 3.61 Banana tree growing on an *Arborloo* pit

Figure 3.62 Planting a mulberry tree on an *Arborloo* pit

citrus, eucalyptus, indigenous and ornamental trees have been tried and are known to respond well. Plant the young tree in a thick layer (15cm) of topsoil placed above the compost. The young trees must be cared for. They must be protected from animals and must be watered often. If the tree dies, plant another. Trees are best planted just before or during the rainy season. In time the tree will provide many fruits, or provide shade or fuel. All growing trees require additional feeding and benefit from the application of leaf compost as a mulch and also garden compost or manure, periodically dug into the topsoil surrounding the tree. Applications of liquid manure also produce a good response. A mug full of wood ash every week or two provides potash which helps fruiting. Nitrogen loving trees like banana also benefit from the addition of urine diluted with water (2 litres urine: 10 litres water), applied once a week.

42 TOILETS THAT MAKE COMPOST

The single pit compost toilet *Arborloo* can be moved about in the garden and will help to make many new trees of various types over the years such as fruit, fuel, building, and shade trees. The time to fill the *Arborloo* pit depends on the depth of the pit and the number of users. It will normally be between 6 and 12 months for small to medium sized families. Space the tree sites to suit the type of tree.

Growing vegetables on *Arborloo* pits

Practical experience has shown that vegetables are also grown on Arborloo pits. In Ethiopia many users of *Arborloos* have chosen to plant pumpkin rather than trees. According to a report by Mayling Simpson-Hebert (2006) the output of pumpkin has been doubled by planting the seeds in *Arborloo* pits (Figure 3.63). Pumpkin has also been planted on Arborloo pits in Mozambique. Sometimes a tree such as banana is planted together with pumpkin on the

Figure 3.63 A pumpkin crop in Ethiopia

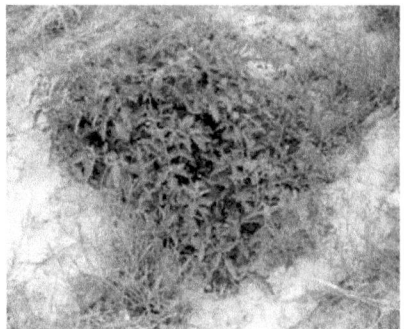

Figure 3.64 Tomato plants growing on an *Arborloo* pit in Zvimba, Zimbabwe

Figure 3.65 Passion fruit growing on an *Arborloo* pit in Malawi

Figure 3.66 Pumpkin growing on a *Fossa alterna* pit in Zimbabwe

same pit. These valuable techniques are also being used in Zimbabwe, where tomato plants are also grown (Figure 3.64). In fact when several *Arborloo* pits are fully composted or in a stage of composting they can be regarded as 'organic oases' with increased fertility and looseness of soil. This is particularly valuable when the surrounding parent soil is poor and contains no humus. Organic fertilizers, compost and manure can also be dug into the organic pit to increase production if desired. Even conventional fertilizers can be added if they are available and affordable to increase the food output of the pit. As experience is gained, the value of these 'agro-pits' may prove to be very useful in the production of a wide range of trees, vegetables and herbs (Figure 3.65 and Figure 3.66). Their safety lies in the fact that the composting material lies beneath a generous layer of topsoil in which the plants start to grow.

Making compost in small single shallow pits

The single pit compost toilet can also be used to make compost for use on the vegetable garden rather than to grow trees. The same structure consisting of a slab, ring beam and toilet house is used and the same method of adding soil and ash to the pit. But the compost must be left in the pit for at least 6 months and preferably 12 months before it is dug out. This means that extra ring beams must be made and pits dug inside them. For the smaller ring beams and slabs three ring beams will be required.

The slab and toilet house will move from the pit 1 to pit 2 and then to pit 3, as the pits fill up with the mix of excreta, soil, ash and leaves. When pit 3 is full, pit 1 is dug out, which should be after roughly 12 months or more of composting. This compost is fertile and can be mixed with garden soil and other compost to grow vegetables. Mix one part compost with two parts topsoil or even mix the two in equal parts. Also, add leaf compost or garden compost if available. The slab and the house can then be put back on pit 1 which has been emptied. So the toilet rotates between the three pits in the garden. The ring beams stay in place permanently. If the larger slab and ring beam is used, then only two ring beams are required for a family unit. This method of alternating between two pits is described in the next chapter.

In this way valuable compost can be harvested from each pit every year, and used to grow better vegetables. It is important that the pit be left for one full year if possible to compost before being dug out. So with our toilet we can also grow trees or we can make good compost for the garden.

The next section deals with making a double pit composting toilet in which only two pits are used. The structure alternates between the two pits at yearly intervals. In fact it is possible to mount both pits inside the same house if the house is large enough, a method which is popular in Malawi and Mozambique.

CHAPTER 4
Fossa alterna – The double pit compost toilet

The double pit compost toilet, *Fossa alterna*, is made up of six parts:

- Two pits
- Two ring beams to protect the two pits
- A single concrete slab which sits on one of the ring beams
- The toilet house which provides privacy

Like the earlier system each pit fills up with a mix of excreta, soil, wood ash and leaves. Leaves are put in the base of the pit before use and every day some soil and wood ash are added to the pit. Dry leaves are also added to the pit. No garbage such as plastic, rags, and bottles is put down the pit. One pit fills up first. During the first season the second pit is unused or is filled with leaves. After the first year the first pit will have filled.

Managing the double pit compost toilet

When the first pit is full, the toilet slab and structure are moved on to the second pit and top soil is placed over the contents of the first pit which is then left to compost. The second pit is then put to use whilst the contents of the first pit are composting. For a small to medium sized family, after a year of use the second pit will be full with excreta, soil, ash and leaves and the first pit will be ready to be emptied of its compost. After the original pit is emptied the toilet slab and structure can be placed back again over the empty pit and the recently filled pit covered with soil and left to compost for a further year. This ritual of changing pits every 12 months can continue for many years in the same site. If the pit filling rate is faster, it is possible to remove pit compost after 6 or 9 months and transfer to a tree pit and plant a tree rather than use on the vegetable garden. The regular addition of soil, ash and leaves to the pit helps the composting process considerably. The system not only provides a valuable toilet facility but also a valuable annual supply of compost for the garden.

Examples of double pit composting toilets

There are many options for making a portable structure. With two rectangular concrete ring beams and slabs, a portable structure can be made of poles and reeds (Figure 4.1) or a steel frame (Figure 4.2). The structure itself can be moved with the slab at yearly intervals in this design.

Figure 4.1 A portable structure using poles and reeds

Figure 4.2 A portable structure using a steel frame

Figure 4.3 A permanent structure housing both pits

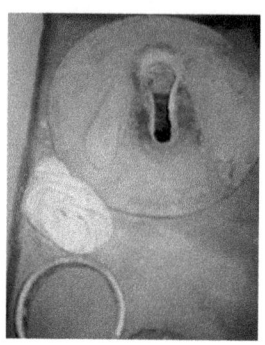

Figure 4.4 Inside of the permanent structure

A permanent structure can also be made for housing the double pit composting toilets. In Malawi and Mozambique, the most popular method of building the *Fossa alterna* is to house both pits within a single superstructure (Figure 4.3). Domed round slabs are often used in Malawi (Figure 4.4). Soil and ash are added to the pit after each use. This helps to control flies and odours and also helps the pit contents to compost faster.

Building the double pit compost toilet

The first step is to make a rectangular concrete slab. The concrete slab is made with a mixture of cement and good quality river sand with some wire reinforcing. The mould for the concrete slab is made from bricks laid on levelled ground.

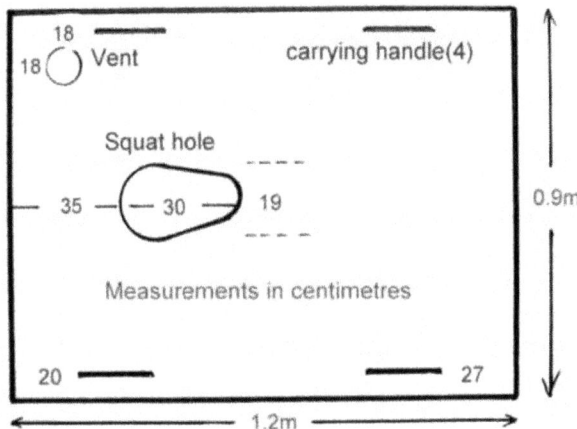

Figure 4.5 Measurements for the 1.2m X 0.9m concrete slab

The slab is 1.2m long and 0.9m wide in this case. It is made by mixing 10 litres of cement with 50 litres of clean river sand. Holes for the squat hole, and vent pipe if required, are made by inserting moulds within the brick mould (Figure 4.5). Half the mix is added to the brick mould first. Eight reinforcing wires – four of 1.15m and four of 0.85m – are laid within the mould. The wire is 3–4mm thick. Then the second half of the mix is added and smoothed down with a wooden float and finally finished with a steel float. Four steel handles can be added if required.

Figure 4.6 shows an example of a slab mould made of bricks and wooden shuttering. The eight pieces of 3mm reinforcing wire have been cut and laid on the plastic ground sheet. Four carrying handles have also been prepared. A 10 litre bucket with the base removed has been shaped by drawing in the two sides with wire. A 75mm length of 110mm pipe has also been cut to make the hole for the vent pipe.

48 TOILETS THAT MAKE COMPOST

Figure 4.6 A slab mould made with bricks and wood

Half the mix is added first, the reinforcing wire is laid, followed by the remaining concrete which is smoothed down. The handles are added by pushing them into the concrete mix (Figure 4.7). A little extra cement can be added around each handle to increase the strength of the concrete at this point. Finally the slab is smoothed down flat with a steel float and left to cure for 7–10 days.

Figure 4.7 The completed slab inside the mould

The next step is to make rectangular concrete ring beams for the double pit compost toilet. In the example described here, the external measurements of the beam are 1.3m x 1.0m and the internal measurements – the size of the hole – are 1.0 x 0.7m (Figure 4.8). This ring beam is made for a slab measuring 1.2m x 0.9m. The mould can be made with bricks. 10 litres of cement are mixed with 50 litres of clean river sand. Half the mix is added first. Wire reinforcing is used within the concrete mix with two strands of

3–4mm wire down each length, making a total of 8 pieces. The total length of wire required is approximately 9 metres. Then the second half of the mix is added and smoothed down with a wooden float. The beam is covered and left to cure for at least 7 days.

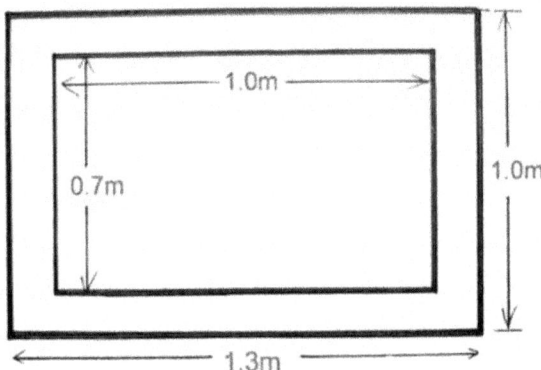

Figure 4.8 A slab mould made with bricks and wood

When constructing the double pit composting toilet, the two ring beams can be cast on the actual toilet site directly on the ground, at least 0.5 metres apart. A level piece of ground, preferably on a slightly elevated site, is best. Alternatively the two ring beams can be cast away from the toilet site and moved on to the site after curing. In this case a plastic sheet should be laid on the ground on which the ring beams can be made. The mould for the ring beam can be made with bricks (Figure 4.9). Wooden shuttering can also be used as a mould, or a combination of bricks and wood. The ring beams are made 75mm thick, about the thickness of a brick. After a few days the bricks can be carefully removed but the watering continues. Note the handles inserted into the ring beam at the edges – these are useful if used with the *Arborloo*, but not necessary with the *Fossa alterna* – since the ring beams will never be moved. In practice handles are rarely used on the ring beam.

Figure 4.9 Ring beam mould using bricks **Figure 4.10** Digging the pit for the *Fossa alterna*

In the case of the *Fossa alterna* the two ring beams can be cast on the site where they will be used about 0.5m apart. In the case of the *Arborloo*, the ring beam is best made offsite and then placed in position as it will be easier to move later. Once the ring beam has been positioned and made level, the soil inside is excavated to the required depth. This is about one metre for the *Arborloo* and between 1.2 and 1.5m for the *Fossa alterna* (Figure 4.10). The excavated soil is deposited around the ring beam and rammed hard. This simple procedure will protect the pit in all but the loosest soils.

Figure 4.11 Adding leaves to the *Fossa alterna* pit **Figure 4.12** Completed *Fossa alterna* pit

Before the slab is fitted it is a very good idea to add a sack of dried leaves to the base of the pit which will be used first (Figure 4.11 and Figure 4.12). This will help the composting process from the moment fresh excreta is added.

This composting process will take longer if the excreta falls on barren soil at the base of the pit. It is also a good idea to fill the second pit with leaves which will make good leaf compost.

The next step is to add the concrete slab (Figure 4.13 and Figure 4.14). Add a layer of weak cement mortar or traditional mortar for the slab to rest on top of the ring beam. This helps the slab to rest on the ring beam without strain. Also if a vent pipe is used, the pit should be air tight, thus allowing the suction of the pipe to draw air down the squat hole or pedestal. This should lead to odourless conditions in the toilet.

Figure 4.13 Addition of the concrete slab

Figure 4.14 The completed pits for the double pit composting toilet

Superstructures with rectangular slabs

The same toilet house superstructure options used for the *Arborloo* can be applied for the *Fossa alterna*. One example is to use a wooden structure and two shallow pits with brick ring beams (Figure 4.15). Another example, from a *Fossa alterna* in a low density suburb in Harare, uses two concrete ring beams and a structure made with a steel frame overlaid by grass and a PVC vent pipe (Figure 4.16).

It is always important to include a hand washing facility. For the hand washing facility shown to the left of the *Fossa alterna* in Figure 4.17, the waste water falls into a flower pot. In the same figure, the second pit is shown filled with leaves and compost during the first year; the second pit was also used to grow comfrey. Inside the toilet house (Figure 4.18) a homemade pedestal has been fitted. The yellow bucket contains a mix of soil and wood ash and a cup for dispensing the mixture. Leaves are also added occasionally.

52 TOILETS THAT MAKE COMPOST

Figure 4.15 *Fossa alterna* using a wooden structure

Figure 4.16 *Fossa alterna* with grass walls

Figure 4.17 *Fossa alterna* at Woodhall Road, Harare

Figure 4.18 Inside a *Fossa alterna* that has been fitted with a pedestal

Figure 4.19 shows the fitting of a portable superstructure to one of the twin *Fossa alterna* pits in Epworth, close to Harare. During the first year the second pit was filled with leaves and soil to make leaf mould. After 12 months the leaf mould was dug out and the slab and structure moved to the second pit. The pit, filled with excreta, soil, ash and leaves, has been topped up with soil (Figure 4.20, right-side).

FOSSA ALTERNA – THE DOUBLE PIT COMPOST TOILET 53

Figure 4.19 Fitting a portable superstructure to a *Fossa alterna* pit

Figure 4.20 A *Fossa alterna* after the second year

Figure 4.21 *Fossa alterna* with a permanent structure

Figure 4.22 Excavating the humus from the pit

Figure 4.23 Digging out compost in Hatcliffe, Zimbabwe

Figure 4.24 Digging out compost in Epworth, Zimbabwe

The *Fossa alterna* can also be enclosed by a permanent structure. This example from Niassa Province, Mozambique (Figure .21) shows the twin pits enclosed in a single pole and grass superstructure which is permanently located. A washing area is also constructed as part of the system. These are very popular units, as they are almost odour and fly-free, unlike many earlier toilets built in the area. They are also relatively low-cost. The pits are each 1.5m deep and protected by brick ring beams. The pits do need to be excavated to use the humus (Figure 4.22, Figure 4.23 and Figure 4.24).

Figure 4.25 Construction of a portable structure for a *Fossa alterna*

Figure 4.26 A *Fossa alterna* with a permanent brick and thatch structure

Figure 4.27 *Fossa alterna* with a metal structure

Figure 4.28 Brick double pit composting toilet

Further examples of structures for the *Fossa alterna* include a portable structure in Kusa Village, Kisumu, Kenya (Figure 4.25), a permanent brick and thatch *Fossa alterna* in Kufunda Village, Ruwa, Zimbabwe (Figure 4.26), a *Fossa alterna* with a metal structure in Maputaland, South Africa (Figure 4.27) and a brick built double pit composting toilet in Lilongwe, Malawi (Figure 4.28).

CHAPTER 5
Low-cost pedestals for simple pit toilets

Pedestals are becoming more popular for use, especially in peri-urban areas. There are several ways of making low-cost pedestals for use in toilets. In each of the methods described here a plastic bucket is used as a mould and insert for the pedestal. The pedestal is built up around in the bucket in cement, which acts as a mould, but also the bucket is left in place to provide a smooth surface inside the pedestal which can be cleaned down.

Very low-cost pedestal

This can be made cheaply from a 10 litre bucket. The base of the ten litre bucket is sawn off and laid wide-end down on a sheet of plastic. A line is drawn around the base rim of the bucket about 75mm out. Strong cement mortar is made of two parts clean river sand and one part cement. This is built up inside the line drawn on the plastic and up against the side walls of the bucket (Figure 5.1). One or two rings of 3mm wire are inserted in the cement for strength. With care this can be done in one sitting.

The pedestal is left to cure for two nights and then the bucket and its concrete surround is lifted up and turned into a base mould made of wood measuring about 40cm x 40cm. The base is cast in 3:1 river sand and cement and left to cure. More thin wire is added in the base for additional strength. The

Figure 5.1 Construction of the very low-cost pedestal

Figure 5.2 Painted very low-cost pedestal

seat is formed by the rim of concrete laid around the bucket on the plastic. It can be shaped and smoothed down with sand paper and once it is dry painted with enamel paint (Figure 5.2). This is really a low-cost but practical method of making a pedestal with easy to wash down plastic insert.

Low-cost pedestal with concrete seat

This method uses a 20 litre bucket and – to reduce cost – a seat made of concrete. In this case a mould is first made in concrete for the seat. This is made by mixing river sand and cement (about 3:1) and building up a toilet seat mould about 50mm deep inside some bricks (dimensions about 50cm x 60cm). The commercially made plastic seat is then pressed into the cement and held down with a weight. It is left there until the concrete is stiff and then the plastic seat can be removed, leaving an impression of the seat. This should be done with care. It may be necessary to finish off the mould with a small trowel to get it smooth. The mould is left to cure for a week, being kept wet at all times. Once cured and dry, it is smoothed down with sand paper.

The mould can now be used to make concrete seats. These are made by taking very thin plastic sheets and covering the seat part of the mould (Figure 5.3). A very strong mix of river sand and cement (2:1) is then used to fill the depression to make the seat. A loop of wire is added to provide strength. L-shaped wire inserts are placed in the concrete to strengthen the link between the seat and the side walls of the pedestal. This is done by laying the wider end of the 20 litre bucket (with the base already sawn off) on the seat. L-shaped pieces of wire are then pushed into the cement around the rim of the bucket. The bucket can be left in place whilst the seat cures. Next a layer of strong cement mortar – two parts river sand and one part cement – is built up around the bucket until it reaches the top (Figure 5.4). This is left to cure overnight and some thin wire is wrapped around the cement work in a spiral form and another layer of cement is applied. This is left to cure for another day or two before the seat and the side walls of the pedestal can be moved. The pedestal, turned right way up, is then mounted within a wooden base mould with outer dimensions of 50cm x 50cm and inner dimensions of 40cm x 40cm. The space between the wooden mould and the side walls of the pedestal are filled with a 3:1 mix of river sand and cement with some wire reinforcing. This is left to cure for another few days being kept wet at all times. Once cured and washed down, the pedestal seat can be sanded down and any small holes filled with pure cement slurry without sand and then allowed to dry. The pedestal is then painted with enamel paint and put to use by cementing in place within the toilet (Figure 5.5 and Figure 5.6).

LOW-COST PEDESTALS FOR SIMPLE PIT TOILETS   57

Figure 5.3 Adding concrete to the toilet seat mould

Figure 5.4 Building up the sides of the bucket

Figure 5.5 Painting the concrete pedestal

Figure 5.6 Finished concrete pedestal

Low-cost pedestal with plastic seat

This is easier to make and smarter, but more expensive. A commercially made plastic toilet seat is required. First holes are made with a hot wire in the supporting plastic ribs under the seat, so that a ring of wire can be threaded through under the seat (Figure 5.7). The hollow under the plastic seat can then be filled with a strong 2:1 river sand and cement mix with the wire inside (Figure 5.8). At the same time a 20 litre bucket (with base sawn off) is placed over the seat in a central position (Figure 5.9) and L-shaped pieces of wire inserted around the rim of the bucket into the cement. This is left to cure for a few hours. Then the side walls of the bucket can be covered with a 2:1 sand and cement mix. This is left to harden a little. Later some thin wire is laid spirally up the side walls of the pedestal to strengthen the unit (Figure 5.10).

58 TOILETS THAT MAKE COMPOST

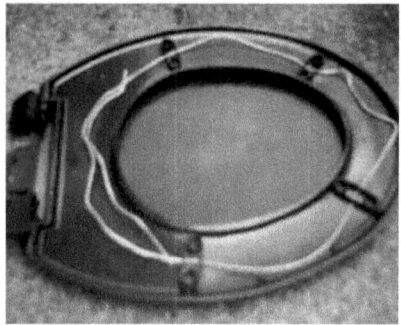

Figure 5.7 Ring of wire added to plastic toilet seat

Figure 5.8 Plastic toilet seat filled with strong concrete

Figure 5.9 Plastic bucket placed over toilet seat

Figure 5.10 Concrete reinforcement added around first layer of concrete

A further layer of mortar is then applied to the side walls. This is left to cure for at least 2 days, being kept wet at all times. The pedestal is then carefully overturned into a base mould made of wood (Figure 5.11), and the base made with more strong concrete and left to cure again. This procedure makes a neat, comfortable and long lasting pedestal (Figure 5.12).

LOW-COST PEDESTALS FOR SIMPLE PIT TOILETS 59

Figure 5.11 Completed pedestal placed in wooden mould

Figure 5.12 Completed low-cost pedestal with plastic seat

CHAPTER 6
Urine-diverting toilets

Urine-diverting toilets use a special pedestal or squat plate in which the urine enters the front part of the pedestal and is then diverted through a pipe and is thus separated from the faeces, which fall directly downwards into a vault or container. Some dry soil and wood ash is added to cover the faeces after every visit. This covers the deposit and helps to dry out the surface of the faeces, and makes them easier to handle and transfer. The distinct advantage of this method is that the urine can be collected separately, making it available as a liquid fertilizer. Also the solid component, being in a semi dry state, is much easier to handle and is safer from the beginning; even if it does initially contain pathogens. Being semi-dry, it does not smell so much and its potential as a fly breeding medium is much reduced, compared to the mix of urine and faeces. Eventually the faeces become completely composted.

There are many types of urine-diverting toilets available for use. Many have double vaults in which one vault is used first and when full the second vault is used. When the second vault is full the first is emptied in the same way as the double pit composting toilet. Meticulous use is rather an essential component of the urine-diverting concept. The pedestals used can either be homemade or commercially made.

The particular urine-diverting toilet described here uses a single vault in which the urine is collected in a plastic container and the faeces, together with soil and ash added to help the composting process, are collected in a 20 litre bucket held in the vault. Once the bucket is nearly full its contents are transferred to a secondary composting site like a cement jar or alternating shallow pit where the ingredients continue to compost for 6–12 months, before being applied to the garden to enhance the quality of vegetable patch soil. When watered, this compost will generate tomatoes by itself from seed passed though the system earlier!

How to build a single vault urine-diverting toilet

The first part of making a single vault urine-diverting toilet is to make the base slab and latrine slab. The base slab is a concrete slab laid on level ground which will form the base of the toilet. The whole structure is built on top of this base slab. A concrete mix is made using five parts clean river sand (50 litres) and one part cement (10 litres). Alternately 3 parts river sand, 2 parts small stones and 1 part cement can be used. The concrete is cast within a mould made of bricks, the dimensions being 1.35m long x 0.9m wide x 75mm deep (Figure 6.1). An area for the step is also made 450mm long and 335mm deep. Some steel reinforcing wires are placed in the concrete. It is left to cure for at least two days before any brickwork is built on top of it. It should be kept wet for several days to cure properly.

Figure 6.1 The brick mould for the base slab

Figure 6.2 The brick mould for the toilet slab

The latrine slab is cast off-site using the same method as for the base slab. The latrine slab is 1.2m long and 0.9m wide and about 40mm deep (Figure 6.2). Holes are cast in the slab for both the pedestal and the vent pipe. A mix of 50 litres clean river sand and 10 litres cement is used. Lengths of reinforcing wire are added after the first half of the concrete mix is added. The second half of the mix is then added and smoothed down with a wooden float followed by a steel float. In fact the same basic slab of 1.2m x 0.9m) can be used to make an *Arborloo*, a *Fossa alterna* or this urine-diverting toilet. Using the same slab it is therefore possible to upgrade the system over time. Money spent on making concrete slabs and other concrete structures is well worth while since they usually last for a lifetime and are a good investment in both money and time.

Making the vault, step and lintel

The vault is built up in fired bricks and mortar to the required height on the base slab (Figure 6.3). If a 20 litre bucket is used the vault should be about 40cm high. This will require about 4 layers of bricks built on edge or about 6 layers built normally. The walls are built so that the outer measurements of the top are 1.2m x 0.9m and the base 1.35m x 0.9m. This allows for the slope at the back of the vault over which the vault access slab at the rear will be fitted (Figure 6.4).

Figure 6.3 Building the vault using bricks on their edge

Figure 6.4 Testing the height of the vault access

Since the rear end of the latrine slab will not be supported on a brick wall it is desirable to make a reinforced concrete lintel which spans the rear end of the vault. This is made with 3 parts river sand and one part cement and reinforced with 3 or 4mm wire. It should be 0.9m long and be 225mm x 75mm wide. Once cured after 7 days it can be carefully mounted on the rear wall of the vault (Figure 6.4).

To make the vault access slab, cast a thin high-strength concrete slab using 2 parts river sand and one part cement with 15mm chicken wire as reinforcing and two wire handles inserted for lifting. The dimensions are about 90cm x 45cm – the exact dimensions must match the vault. This is cured for 7–10 days and will be rested against the sloping rear side of the vault (Figure 6.5). A neat, almost airtight fit is required. This is made by applying strong cement plaster to the vault brickwork and grease to the adjacent cement panel side and bringing the two together. After curing the panel can be withdrawn leaving an exact impression on the vault. The concrete toilet slab is then fitted and bonded on top of the vault in cement mortar (Figure 6.6).

Figure 6.5 Fitting the vault access slab

Figure 6.6 Front view of the vault with the toilet slab placed on top

The urine-diverting pedestal

Urine-diverting pedestals can be homemade, purchased commercially or modified from commercial non urine-diverting pedestals which are more commonly available. Homemade urine-diverting pedestals can be made from off-the-shelf plastic buckets and cement. There are several methods of constructing urine-diverting pedestals, with the example shown here as only one such method. The 20 litre plastic bucket forms the inner shell of the pedestal and is attached to a standard plastic toilet seat. These are bonded together within a shell of cement mortar. Part of the bucket base is used to make the urine diversion section. The urine passes out of the urine diverter through a plastic elbow and plastic pipe. This can be led to a tree, soakaway or a plastic urine storage container. In this case the urine off-take lies above the pedestal base, which means the unit can be mounted on an ecological pit toilet as well as an above-the-ground vault.

Sequence of making a homemade urine-diverting pedestal with urine outlet pipe above slab level

The material requirements are a 20 litre plastic bucket, a 20mm polyethylene bend, a plastic toilet seat and cement, sand and wire (Figure 6.7). First the base is sawn off the bucket squarely (Figure 6.8). Next, the plastic base of the bucket is sawn in two (Figure 6.9 and Figure 6.10); one of these halves will be used to make the urine diverter within the bucket. The half base is fitted within the bucket about half way up the walls at an angle (Figure 6.11). It is secured in place by drilling small holes through cut base and bucket walls and passing wire through and tightening (Figure 6.12). A hole is drilled through the bucket wall just above the base of the urine diverter. The 20mm polyethylene bend is fitted through the hole and turned at an angle on the outside (Figure 6.13 and Figure 6.14).

The next step is to make the seat. Using a hot wire, holes are drilled through the plastic ribs which support the seat (Figure 6.15). These allow a wire to be threaded in a loop under the seat (Figure 6.16). A strong mix of concrete, using 3 parts river sand and 1 part cement, is mixed and added to the toilet seat (Figure 6.17). This will add strength to the seat and form a bond between the seat and side walls of the pedestal. The bucket is now fitted centrally over the toilet seat, with the urine-diverting hold facing the front of the toilet seat (Figure 6.18). Eight pieces of bent wire are now introduced into the cement supporting the seat (Figure 6.19). This is allowed to cure overnight. Next a further mix of 3:1 sand and cement is made and plastered half way up the walls of the bucket (Figure 6.20). This is left overnight again to cure.

The following morning the upper half of the bucket is cemented with a 3:1 mix (Figure 6.21) and allowed to cure overnight. The next morning the bucket and seat are overturned into a base mould made with wood, about 60cm x

Figure 6.7 Materials for the homemade urine-diverting toilet pedestal

Figure 6.8 Cutting the base off the bucket

Figure 6.9 Marking the plastic base

Figure 6.10 The cut plastic base

60cm and 40mm deep (Figure 6.22). It is laid over a plastic sheet.

The base mould is filled with the same 3:1 river sand and cement mix. Some wire is added to the base. Also some thin wire is also coiled around the pedestal (Figure 6.23). Next a final layer of 3:1 mix is plastered up the side walls of the pedestal over the wire. The final layer can be made with cement watered down to make a thick paint and is applied with a brush. This is allowed to cure for several days being kept wet at all times (Figure 6.24). It is covered with plastic sheet and sacking.

The space between the bucket side wall and urine diverter is now sealed. Any type of pliable putty can be used for this job. Even chewing gum will do. It is pressed into the gap from underneath first (Figure 6.25). The putty should also be pressed into the gap from the upper side too (Figure 6.26). Urine passing into the urine diverter should find its way through the plastic bend and through the plastic pipe. The urine outlet pipe is added to the polyethylene pipe bend (Figure 6.27). This is led back over the concrete base of the urine-diverting pedestal to the rear of the toilet (Figure 6.28). The pedestal can be made more attractive by coating with enamel paint once the concrete is completely cured and dry (Figure 6.29 and Figure 6.30). Once dry it can be mounted into the toilet slab. The urine-diverting pedestal can be fitted into a single or double-vault dehydrating or composting toilet (Figure 6.31). It can also be fitted over a shallow pit toilet. The urine pipe can be led into a soakaway or into a vegetable garden, preferably beneath ground level. The urine can also be led to a plastic container placed in a hole dug in the ground. The pipe can also be led to a tree, such as a banana tree (Figure 6.32).

URINE-DIVERTING TOILETS 67

Figure 6.11 The cut base fitted half-way up the bucket at an angle

Figure 6.12 Attaching the cut base with wire

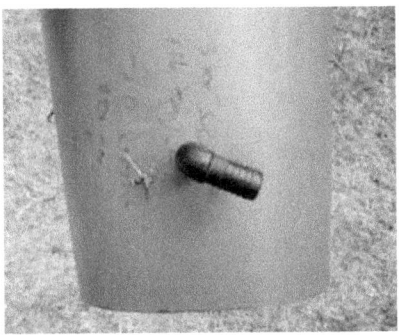

Figure 6.13 Fitting of the pipe bend to the bucket

Figure 6.14 Inside view of the fitted pipe bend

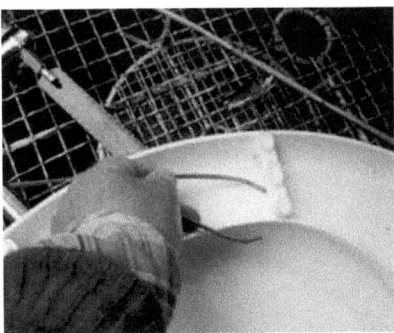

Figure 6.15 Using a hot wire to make a hole through the plastic toilet seat ribs

Figure 6.16 The toilet seat with a threaded loop of wire

68 TOILETS THAT MAKE COMPOST

Figure 6.17 Concrete added to the toilet seat

Figure 6.18 Bucket placed onto the toilet seat

Figure 6.19 Bent wire added around the bucket

Figure 6.20 Concrete added half-way up the bucket

Figure 6.21 Upper-half of bucket covered in concrete

Figure 6.22 Bucket and seat turned over and placed into base mould

URINE-DIVERTING TOILETS 69

Figure 6.23 Wire added for reinforcement

Figure 6.24 Completed pedestal curing

Figure 6.25 Sealing the urine diverter against the bucket wall

Figure 6.26 Sealing the top side of the urine diverter

Figure 6.27 Urine outlet pipe attached

Figure 6.28 Outlet pipe led to the back of the toilet

70 TOILETS THAT MAKE COMPOST

Figure 6.29 Painting the pedestal

Figure 6.30 Close-up of the base of the pedestal

Figure 6.31 Urine-diverting pedestal installed

Figure 6.32 Exterior of toilet house with urine-diverting toilet

Making a simple urine-diverting platform

The pedestal toilet is not the only low-cost option available for a urine-diverting toilet. Figure 6.33 and Figure 6.34 show a homemade copy of the excellent Chinese urine-diverting squatting platform. A ten litre bucket is cut and fitted with a pipe and mounted at a slight angle in a high strength concrete slab cast with two holes. This is fitted over the main toilet slab. Urine is diverted into the bucket and drains through the outlet pipe. It is best the unit be painted with enamel paint.

Urine-diverting toilet installation details

For any urine-diverting system where the urine is led through the pipe to a tree or vegetable garden, it is possible to add more water through the urine diverter to cleanse the pipe and dilute the urine. When the diverter is used over a shallow pit, it is advisable to add soil and ash to cover the deposit to encourage composting and reduce flies and odours. If composting is required in the pit, the pit contents must be moistened by adding some urine or water, with soil and ash, and preferably leaves. Composting cannot take place in a completely dry system.

Figure 6.33 Top-view of a urine-diverting squat toilet

Figure 6.34 Side-view of a urine-diverting squat toilet

Figure 6.35 Urine-diverting pedestal with a handsome wooden seat

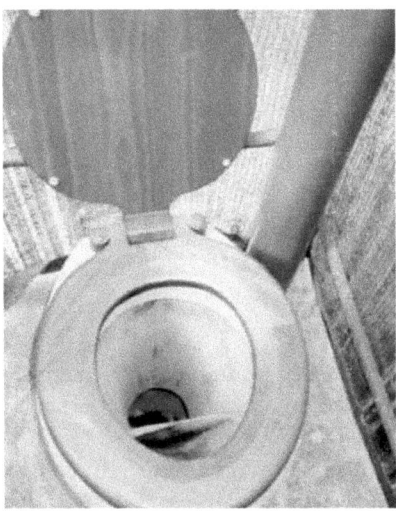

Figure 6.36 Top-view of the a urine-diverting pedestal

72 TOILETS THAT MAKE COMPOST

Style and design are an important part of the toilet. Figure 6.35 and Figure 6.36 show a urine-diverting pedestal with a modified toilet chute and fitted with a comfortable wooden seat. Note also the vent pipe fitted behind the pedestal to the right. The vent helps to aerate the vault, removing odours and excess moisture. The vent pipe can be made with 110mm PVC pipe.

Pedestals are mounted over the hole in the slab and cement mortared in position. It is important that this joint is watertight, so that any water falling on the slab from rain or washing water does not drip into the bucket below which must contain faeces, paper, soil and wood ash only and absolutely no water.

Urine is a valuable plant food and is best collected in a container. The best method is to build an extra brick side-chamber on one side of the vault. This will house a plastic container of about 20 litres capacity which will receive and store the urine. A plastic pipe is led from the urine outlet of the pedestal through the side wall of the vault into the brick side chamber so that the urine can be caught by a small funnel which directs it into the urine storage container (Figure 6.37 and Figure 6.38). The brickwork of the side chamber is built up to enclose and protect the container and the piping. The side vault is built up on soil so that any urine overflow can drain away. The chamber is covered with a concrete lid with handles.

Figure 6.37 The brick mould for the base slab

Figure 6.38 The brick mould for the toilet slab

It is important to ensure that the plastic pipe leading from the urine outlet to the container falls continuously and does not pass through a loop which will act as a water trap or air lock. The side wall chamber must be big enough to house the container so that it can easily be withdrawn. Since urine is very corrosive, the piping and container must be made of stout plastic. Metal parts will corrode. Figure 6.39 shows a finished structure with side vault for urine collection.

Figure 6.39 Side-vault for urine collection

Figure 6.40 Internal view of vault with plastic bucket placed for collection of faeces

Make sure the rear access door fits well at the rear of the vault. The vent pipe will function better if the vault is well sealed. Two bricks can be mortared on the base slab to locate the best position for the bucket which is directly under the pedestal. A 20 litre bucket has been fitted within the vault (Figure 6.40). The vent pipe is fitted into the toilet slab and through the roof. A latch is fitted to the door to hold it closed. A mix of dry soil and dry wood ash (4:1) is provided in a container. It is best to mix bulk dry soil and ash first and hold in a sack, or dust bin, then bring to the toilet in small lots.

Urine-diverting superstructures

Many types of superstructure are possible for urine-diverting toilets. They are built in one location and thus can be made from bricks or timber, metal sheeting, asbestos sheeting, reeds, grass or of any material that offers privacy. In this case, the vent pipe is placed within the structure and the roof must have a hole made for the ventilation pipe to pass through. Structures are fitted with a door of some sort. A roof is essential as this prevents rain water entering the interior and the pedestal. Water must not be allowed to penetrate into the vault.

One example of a superstructure uses a frame of polyethylene pipes covered with plastic shade cloth (Figure 6.41). This is not very robust but has proved very adequate over a four year period. The urine-diverting pedestal is smart and comfortable. A mixture of soil and wood ash (4:1) is stored in one container, with dispenser. Toilet paper is held in another container. Another example of a superstructure is a brick single-vault urine-diverting toilet built by Mvuramanzi Trust (Figure 6.42).

74 TOILETS THAT MAKE COMPOST

Figure 6.41 Superstructure made of polyethylene pipes covered with a plastic cloth

Figure 6.42 A brick single-vault urine-diverting toilet

Use and management of the urine-diverting toilet

Since the faeces from the urine-diverting toilet will be used to make humus, it is essential that soil and wood ash are added after every visit to the latrine. The bucket then fills up with a mixture of materials which compost easily – faeces, paper, soil and wood ash. It is wise to premix the soil and the ash when these materials are in the dry state at a ratio of four parts soil to one part ash. This can be stored for use in a larger container or sack, and brought and stored in smaller containers within the toilet. The ash and soil can be applied down the chute using a small cup or homemade dispenser made from the upper part of a plastic milk bottle. Half a cupful of the mix is added after every deposit made. When the bucket of contents is nearly full, its contents are transferred to a secondary composting site for further processing. The rate of filling depends on the number of users and the amount of soil and ash added. Weekly transferral may be required for a family of about six. For a single user, the bucket may take 4–6 weeks to fill up. The urine accumulates in the plastic container until it is nearly full. This urine can be used in various ways (see Chapter 11).

Processing the faeces

The faeces (without urine) fall directly into the bucket, and it is wise to put some humus or leaves in the base when it is empty to avoid sticking and to help start the composting process off. In this unit the bucket is removed and its contents transferred to a secondary processing site quite regularly. The frequency of moving the bucket and its contents depends on how quickly the bucket fills up and this is related to the number of users. In this toilet fresh excreta does not remain in the toilet system itself for long. It may be just a few days or a week or two at most. Thus in practice the toilet can be considered the primary processing site, in so far that the ingredients are placed together and start to change their form, but the period is brief. When the bucket is nearly full, the rear vault access slab is removed and the bucket withdrawn (Figure 6.43) and its contents tipped into a secondary composting site nearby (Figure 6.44 and Figure 6.45). The secondary composting site can be a shallow pit composter or a split cement jar. A 30 litre split cement jar is ideal for processing human faeces. Fertile soil is added on top of the excreta and a strong lid placed over the top for protection. More deposits are made when the bucket fills again. After 3 or 4 months the contents are pleasant to handle. Naturally it is always wise to wash hands after handling humus of any type, including this variety. Some soil is placed back into the empty bucket and then it is placed back in the vault beneath the pedestal. The rear vault slab is replaced and the toilet can be used again. The transferral of materials from primary to secondary composting sites is quick and easy.

The secondary composting site is where the raw excreta is converted into a product which is best called humus. The humus has the appearance of loam-like soil and smells pleasant. These sites include shallow pits (tree pit or fertility pit, or twin shallow pits), trenches, compost heaps and also buckets

Figure 6.43 Removal of bucket of faeces

Figure 6.44 Emptying the bucket of faeces into the secondary composting site

76 TOILETS THAT MAKE COMPOST

Figure 6.45 Emptying faeces into a small shallow pit

Figure 6.46 Cement jars for composting faeces

or split cement jars, where the composting process can take place. Plastic bags have also been used. The tree pit is a shallow pit covered with a lid into which the bucket contents are placed and then covered up with fertile soil. When the pit is almost full it is topped up with a good layer of topsoil and a young tree is planted in the topsoil. This works like the *Arborloo* – in fact this method preceded the *Arborloo* which evolved from it. A similar method is used with a trench, which is filled up in stages with buckets of the mixed composting ingredients.

Amongst these various techniques the author has predominantly used the method of processing the faeces in split cement jars (Figure 6.46). This is a highly effective and adaptable method and has the advantage that the forming humus can be exposed by dividing the split jar – taking off one of the two jar shells. Over the years this has been one of the best demonstration tools for promoting recycling and ecological sanitation, as visitors can see the humus and it is very convincing.

Stages of building a twin pit composter for a single vault urine-diverting toilet

Choose a level site near the toilet and cast two ring beams from concrete on the ground (Figure 6.47). The internal measurement is variable but in the case shown here the internal measurement was 0.8m x 0.8m. The width of the ring beam was 15cm and the depth 7.5cm. A mix of 5 parts river sand and 1 part cement was used. The two ring beams were placed about 0.75m apart. The concrete was allowed to cure for a period of 3 days under a plastic sheet. After curing, the bricks and timber shuttering have been removed from the ring beam and each filled with water to loosen the soil beneath (Figure 6.48).

After a day and night soaking the soil is easier to dig. The two pits should be dug down to about 0.5m metres (Figure 6.49). The soil removed from the twin pits has been laid around the ring beams and rammed in place. This makes the pits more stable. The pit which will not be used first can be filled with leaves to compost (Figure 6.50), whilst the other pit will be filled with a mix of faeces, paper, soil and ash from the toilet. The area around the ring beams is smoothed down and made neat.

A wooden lid is made for the twin pit composter and placed over the pit which is being filled with excreta, soil, paper and ash (Figure 6.51 and Figure 6.54). The almost full bucket (Figure 6.52) is removed from the toilet vault and tipped into the shallow pit (Figure 6.53). The deposit is covered with more soil and leaves.

Figure 6.47 Casting ring beams

Figure 6.48 Cured ring beams

Figure 6.49 Dug-out pits

Figure 6.50 Twin pits ready for use with right-side pit filled with leaves

78 TOILETS THAT MAKE COMPOST

Figure 6.51 Wooden lid for active composting pit

Figure 6.52 Bucket of faeces ready for emptying

Figure 6.53 Emptying the bucket of faeces into the pit

Figure 6.54 Active composting pit covered by wooden lid

Many more buckets of faeces will be added until the pit is almost full. Since the excreta is close to the soil – and is surrounded by soil – and the additions of soil and leaves are made in small amount, the composting process is quite efficient. The pits are called secondary composting sites because the actual composting process starts off in the bucket itself and the process continues in the shallow pits. Leaves help a lot to accelerate the composting process in the shallow pit. These add more air into the system and also organisms which help to break down the excreta. The final humus is more crumbly in texture if leaves have been added. Water is added periodically to keep the composting ingredients damp. The two pits are used alternately. Once the first pit has filled up, which should take rather more than 6 months, the second pit is put to use. When the second pit is full, the first pit can be emptied and the process started again on the original pit. Once the compost is fully formed in the pit

URINE-DIVERTING TOILETS 79

it can be dug out and used on vegetable gardens and flower beds. It can also be mixed with very poor soil to enhance the growth of vegetables.

Routine maintenance of the urine-diverting toilet

Routine cleaning and maintenance of the urine-diverting toilet is important for the best functioning of the unit. This is not an arduous task and can be carried out quickly once every month or two. Urine-diverting pedestals have no means of flushing down the sidewalls and it is inevitable that some fouling will take place. Whilst the vent will carry any odours down into the vault and up the pipe, periodic cleansing of the chute is desirable. During normal use, the dry soil and ash mix will cover any side wall fouling; dry it out, and make it less objectionable.

The great advantage of the urine-diverting system described here, where the faeces are contained in a removable bucket and not a static vault, is that the system can be washed down completely once the bucket and the urine container have been removed. It is desirable that the vent pipe, pedestal and urinal pipe are washed down and cleaned from time to time. First the bucket and urine container are removed and put to one side. The vent pipe, which will normally be made of PVC, is also pulled out. Cobwebs which may have developed in the vent can then be cleaned out with a small tree branch. The whole vent can then be thoroughly washed down and cleaned out with water. The pedestal is cleaned entirely from top to bottom including the side walls with water. The urine pipe is also flushed out with water. The toilets, floors and vault can also be washed down with water.

It is important to thoroughly clean out the ventilation pipe from time to time to retain its efficiency. This is because spiders weave their webs inside the pipe and this seriously disrupts the air flow inside the pipe (Figure 6.55

Figure 6.55 Spider webs inside the vault

Figure 6.56 Spider webs and spiders inside the vault

80   TOILETS THAT MAKE COMPOST

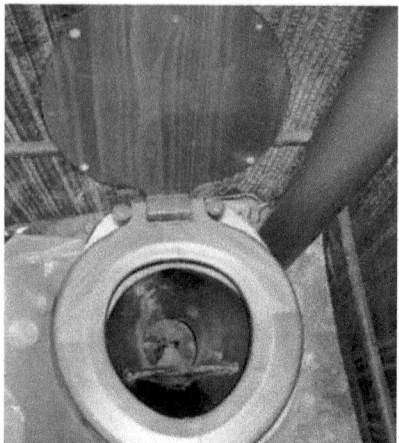 

Figure 6.57 Cleaned urine-diverting toilet

Figure 6.58 Wild basil *Ocimum canum*, a mosquito repellent

and Figure 6.56). Efficient ventilation is important and helps to reduce odours and also maintains a constant flow of air through the vault which reduces moisture.

The toilet and its parts are then allowed to dry out and are all put back together including the bucket, urine container and vent (Figure 6.57). The dry soil and ash container inside the toilet is constantly being refilled from a larger stored stock elsewhere. During the wet season, it has been found that Culicine mosquitoes, which do not carry malaria, can hide in the vault and emerge up the pedestal chute during use. The mosquitoes look for dark places to hide but they do not breed there as there is no water. Attempts at controlling these mosquitoes have been made by introducing sprigs of the wild basil *Ocimum canum* (Figure 6.58), which is know to be a mosquito repellent. Flies have never been seen in this system.

CHAPTER 7
Upgrading the toilet system

The basic concept behind upgrading the toilet system is to start simple and improve it over time. The *Arborloo* is an excellent entry point for householders who wish to consider using ecological toilets and recycle their excreta. It is simple, cheap and the excreta is never touched. But the *Arborloo* can be upgraded to a *Fossa alterna* and this is a trend which is being followed in several programmes. Also toilets can be upgraded by fitting pedestals and vent pipes. The advantages of upgrading an *Arborloo* to a *Fossa alterna* are the permanence of location and a regular supply of compost. It is also possible to upgrade the *Fossa alterna* (or even *Arborloo*) to urine diversion (Figure 7.1). This brings with it extra costs and complexity. But the pit contents will be drier, with less potential for odour and fly breeding. Also the urine can be led to a sunken plastic container for collection. The urine can also be led to a seepage area planted with a nitrogen hungry tree, such as a banana tree, or a garden compost pit or some other seepage area. The pit contents will be drier which will be an advantage especially if the soil does not drain well. In those cases where a urine-diverting pedestal is fitted to a shallow pit composting system, it is best that the urine pipe is led off above the base of the pedestal (Figure 7.2). Underground piping can be difficult to fit to pit structures. The same urine diverter, often using the same concrete slab, can be fitted to a brick vault where the toilet is constructed entirely above ground level.

Upgrading using a round slab and ring beam

The 1.0m diameter concrete slab and matching ring beam can be made cheaply and is normally used to construct an *Arborloo*. But just as the same slab can be used on a *Fossa alterna* system, the same concrete slab and ring beam can also be used to make a urine-diverting toilet. The ring beam has been laid down on level ground and backfilled with soil (Figure 7.3). A round brick wall is then built up on the ring beam to form a vault, with an opening at the rear, and high enough to accept a 20 litre bucket for containing the faeces, ash and soil (Figure 7.4).

A one metre diameter slab is then fitted and bonded on top of the round vault in cement mortar and a urine-diverting pedestal fitted (Figure 7.5). This could also be a squatting type urine-diverting platform. A concrete vault

82　TOILETS THAT MAKE COMPOST

Figure 7.1　Urine-diverting pedestal fitted to a Fossa alterna system

Figure 7.2　Urine off-take fitted above the base of the pedestal

Figure 7.3　Ring beam laid on level ground

Figure 7.4　Brick wall built-up on ring beam

Figure 7.5　Slab and pedestal fitted on built-up base

Figure 7.6　Concrete vault access door

UPGRADING THE TOILET SYSTEM   83

Figure 7.7 Structure around upgraded toilet

Figure 7.8 Urine-diverting pipe attached to base of pedestal

access door has also been made and fitted to the rear of the vault (Figure 7.6). A simple structure (Figure 7.7) is then built around the vault for privacy and the urine pipe is led off to a banana plant close by (Figure 7.8). Structures can also be upgraded.

Upgrading using a rectangular slab

An *Arborloo* (Figure 7.9) or a *Fossa alterna* (Figure 7.10) built using a rectangular concrete slab can be upgraded following the same method as for the round slab. Most *Arborloo* and *Fossa alterna* toilets use squat holes rather than pedestals but they can be upgraded by adding pedestals and vent pipes. The vent pipe helps to remove smells and excess moisture from the pit.

Figure 7.9 Arborloo built on a rectangular slab

Figure 7.10 Fossa alterna built on a rectangular slab

84 TOILETS THAT MAKE COMPOST

The upgrading can be done gradually. A *Fossa alterna*, using a 1.2m x 0.9m slab, can be upgraded first by adding a non urine-diverting pedestal (Figure 7.11) and later by adding a urine-diverting pedestal (Figure 7.12). When fitted to a shallow pit system the urine-diverting pedestal is easier to install if the urine pipe lies above slab level. When the urine-diverting pedestal has been mounted on a 1.2m x 0.9m concrete slab mounted on an above-ground vault (Figure 7.13), the urine pipe can be led off below slab level to a soakaway or plastic storage container. Figure 7.14 shows both the urine pipe located below the slab and the two bricks cemented to the base that help locate the faeces bucket directly below the toilet.

Figure 7.11 Fossa alterna upgraded with a non urine-diverting pedestal

Figure 7.12 Fossa alterna upgraded with a urine-diverting pedestal

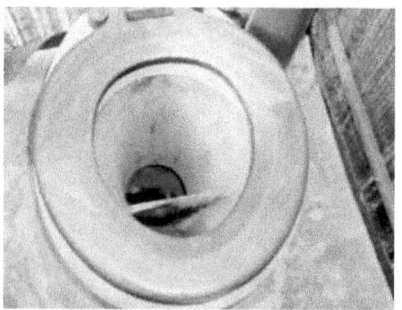

Figure 7.13 Urine-diverting pedestal mounted above the ground

Figure 7.14 Urine pipe located below the slab

CHAPTER 8
Odour and fly control

The control of insects and odour are important issues to deal with in improved toilet facilities. The elimination of odours makes the toilet far more pleasant to use, and the control of insects, particularly flies, is important for health reasons. Too many flies are also a nuisance.

Odour control

A screened ventilation pipe can reduce odours and flies in all the compost-making toilets described in this book. The vent pipe draws out air from the pit or vault, mostly by the action of air passing across the top of the pipe (Figure 8.1). One option for the vent pipe material is to use 110mm PVC. The air that flows out of the pipe is replaced by air passing down the squat hole or pedestal. This is most efficient when the slab and pit collar are sealed and airtight and the head of the pipe is not surrounded by trees. Any foul odour from the pit or vault does not escape into the superstructure, but is diluted by air and passes out of the pipe into the atmosphere. The effect is that the toilet becomes almost odourless. The vent also helps to remove moist air from the pit or vault which helps to reduce the moisture content of the excreta.

Also a urine-diverting pedestal which separates urine from faeces (Figure 8.2) will also have the effect of reducing odours, since the faeces are drier when not mixed with urine. The drying effect is increased by adding wood ash or dry soil to the deposit. This will also control flies.

But PVC pipes and urine-diverting pedestals may be too expensive to fit to very low-cost pit toilets. In this case the regular addition of soil, wood ash and leaves to the pit will help to reduce odour. Keeping the toilet clean and covering the squat hole can also help. It is possible to upgrade a simple pit toilet by adding a vent pipe or urine-diverting pedestal or both at a later date. The urine-diverting pedestal should ideally be one where the urine off-take is above slab level. This makes plumbing arrangements on pit toilets easier.

86 TOILETS THAT MAKE COMPOST

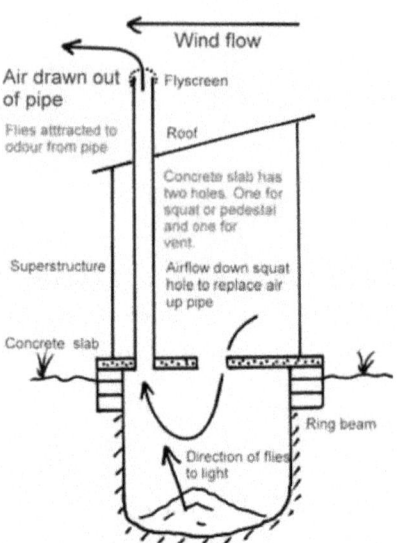

Figure 8.1   The effect of a vent pipe

Figure 8.2   Urine-diverting pedestal

Fly control

In urine-diverting toilets, the faeces are deposited separately and covered with dry soil and ash. Flies do not breed well under these conditions. But if soil and ash are not added, fly breeding can begin. However fly breeding is easier to control in urine-diverting toilets, simply by adding more dry ash and dry soil to the deposit. It is essential that the urine-diverting vault is not flooded with water or urine added. This will make things very messy. User education is required on the proper use and maintenance of urine-diverting toilets.

The method used in the ventilated improved pit (VIP) latrine effectively controls flies as well as odours if the conditions are met, such as fitting a screened vent pipe. Corrosion resistant aluminium or stainless steel screens must be used. The toilet house must be kept in semi-darkness and a roof is essential. Open doors allow flies to escape through the house. Where the interior of the toilet is kept semi-dark, flies will enter the pipe from the pit or vault and become trapped by the screen. This is because flies are attracted to light when they leave the pit and enter the pipe, which is the most obvious light source. From the outside, flies are attracted by odours coming from the pit or vault and most of these are expelled through the head of the vent. If the head of the pipe is screened, flies cannot enter the pit. This simple effect can dramatically reduce fly breeding in the pit toilet or vault and thus reduce the

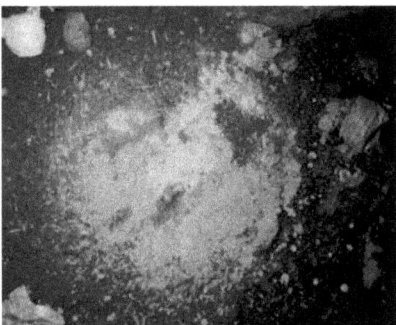

Figure 8.3 Addition of wood ash to the pit to control fly breeding

passage of fly-born disease. This is the principle of the VIP toilet. Fly breeding will also be reduced if the pit contents are drier. Thus adding a urine-diverting pedestal to a shallow pit system will help.

For lower cost shallow pit composting toilets a vent pipe or urine-diverting pedestal may also be too expensive to fit. Then fly breeding, which is a natural phenomenon in pit toilets, must be controlled by some other means. This is because the mix of faeces and urine is far more fluid than faeces alone produced in urine-diverting toilets. Flies breed most in pits which are moist and also during the warm wet season in Southern Africa, from December to March. The liberal addition of wood ash is known to reduce the potential for fly breeding in pit toilets (Figure 8.3) but it may not eliminate them altogether. So if flies build up, it helps to add ash liberally if it is available, especially during the hotter, wetter months when the fly problem is worst. The liberal addition of ash will also reduce odours. Where soil, ash and leaves are added in combination, the pit gets a mix of soil organisms, potash and composting matter which helps to make better pit compost for later use in agriculture and tree growing. So the more of these additional materials is added the better the final compost and the greater the degree of fly and odour control. The pit filling time is reduced as more soil, ash and leaves are added and a balance must be struck between adding too much or too little. In rural projects, homesteaders are often reluctant to add too much soil or ash at first, but soon learn that flies and odours are controlled better if more is added.

CHAPTER 9
A matter of hygiene and hand washing

Hand washing facilities are vital if any hygienic value can be expected out of a toilet system. Hand washing is perhaps the most vital part of the process of improving personal hygiene. In fact hand washing is essential if an improved state of health is to be achieved in relation to toilet use. All eco-toilets (and any other toilet) should be fitted with a simple hand washing device as a matter of priority. There are many ways of making simple hand washing devices. The simplest is described below. The use of pot racks to hygienically dry out plates and pots is also useful. Cleanliness within the home is vital if the best health is to be gained. A simple but healthy diet also helps.

Simple hand washing devices

Hand washing devices can be made very simply and at almost no cost. Three simple types of hand washing device are described here. The first two originate in Malawi where they are used in both the CCAP and COMWASH ecosan programmes. Both use a plastic cup (Figure 9.1) or a tin/aluminium can (Figure 9.3) with two or three 3mm holes drilled or punched near the base. A nail could also be used to make the holes. In the first case the cup or can is suspended with string from either the toilet itself or from a simple wooden structure near the toilet. Plants can be grown below the hand washing device so that the used water is not wasted (Figure 9.2). Water is taken from a nearby basin or bucket with a cup or scoop and poured into the device just prior to washing. Water can also be held in a plastic bottle nearby and poured into the device (Figure 9.5). In the second case the tin can is attached to a length of wire and suspended from this wire. At the time of hand washing the tin can is held by the wire, dipped in a container of water, and then hung up again. The water drains out for hand washing (Figure 9.4). Even a single hole will provide enough water for hand washing (Figure 9.6). A bar of soap can also be suspended nearby. Hard soap is best since a hole can be drilled through the soap and suspended on a string near the hand washing device (Figure 9.7). These simple hand washers can be made in minutes, cost almost nothing and can cleanse the hands of dangerous bacteria after toilet use.

The second type of simple hand washing device is made from a round plastic bottle with screw cap. Any size will do but the larger the bottle, the

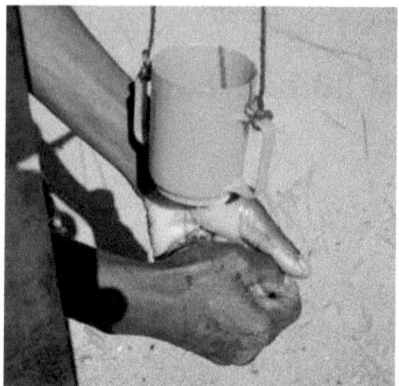

Figure 9.1 A simple plastic cup hand washing device

Figure 9.2 Used water falls on to plants below

Figure 9.3 A simple tin can hand washing device

Figure 9.4 Using the tin can hand washing device

more hand washes can be made before refilling is necessary. A short length of 3mm steel wire is taken and a point filed down on one end. The used bottle is filled with water and a hole pierced near the bottom with the wire (Figure 9.8). It may help to wrap some cloth around the wire to hold it firmly. The wire is pushed though the plastic and withdrawn. When the cap is screwed up water will not come out of the hole (Figure 9.9). When the cap is unscrewed water will come out of the hole, sufficient for hand washing (Figure 9.10). The device is hung up near the toilet. Put more in the bathroom, kitchen and eating areas. As with the first hand washing device, a bar of soap can also be suspended nearby.

Hand washers should be fitted to every toilet made. In fact several should be mounted around the homestead at convenient places. It should always be used prior to eating or handling food. Regular hand washing is vital

Figure 9.5 Adding water to the tin can

Figure 9.6 Tin can with a single hole

Figure 9.7 Tin can and a bar of soap

Figure 9.8 Piercing a hole in the plastic bottle

Figure 9.9 Putting-on the screw cap

Figure 9.10 Open screw cap for hand washing

if improvements to health in water and sanitation programmes are to be effective. It is remarkable that something so simple and cheap to make can be so valuable.

CHAPTER 10
How to use toilet compost in the garden

Toilet compost varies a great deal in texture and colour depending on the amount and type of soil added. Where sandy soil has been added, the toilet compost is sandy and almost humus-free (Figure 10.1). On the upper right of Figure 10.1, some dried out fly cocoons have been separated-off, proof that this material was once excreta. Where fertile soil and leaves have been added, the toilet compost is much more humus-like (Figure 10.2). The humus-like sample has also been sieved making it an excellent potting soil for planting seedlings.

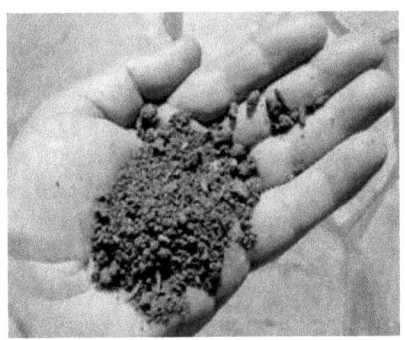

Figure 10.1 Sandy toilet compost   **Figure 10.2** Humus-like toilet compost

The demonstration that human excreta can change into these soils and humus can be an important step in convincing people that something good can come out of practicing ecosan. Figure 10.3 shows toilet compost recently dug out of the pit of a Fossa alterna. When fully composted, toilet compost is pleasant to handle and safe to use (Figure 10.4). It can greatly enhance the fertility of very poor soils and can also be used as a potting soil or added to vegetable and flower beds. Toilet compost taken from urine-diverting toilets is an excellent medium for growing tomatoes. Pit compost taken from the double pit compost toilet can have a dramatic enhancing effect on very poor sandy soil. In this example, the very poor topsoil was mixed with an equal volume of pit compost: 5 litres plus 5 litres. The increase in growth is very significant. Poor soils, such as those used in the trial, are very common in Africa. By adding toilet compost to poor soil, vegetable production can be enhanced significantly.

Figure 10.3 Toilet compost dug out of a *Fossa alterna* pit

Figure 10.4 Inspecting the toilet compost

Testing crops in toilet pit compost

A test crop of spinach grown on poor soil was compared to spinach grown in the same poor soil mixed with an equal volume of pit compost. After 30 days of growth, the harvest was increased 7 times (Figure 10.5) for the enhanced soil. The same growth test was done with covo grown on poor soil compared to covo grown on the same poor soil mixed with an equal volume of pit compost. After 30 days of growth, the harvest was increased 4 times (Figure 10.6).
For the lettuce growth test in poor and enhanced soil, after 30 days of growth

Figure 10.5 Spinach growth test - the bucket on the right has soil enhanced with toilet compost

Figure 10.6 Covo growth test – the bucket on the right has soil enhanced with toilet compost

the harvest was increased 7 times (Figure 10.7). The onion growth test in poor and enhanced soil produced similar results, with a harvest increase of nearly 3 times after four months of growth (Figure 10.8). In all of these examples, the use of urine would have enhanced the production further.

Figure 10.7 Lettuce growth test - the bucket on the right has soil enhanced with toilet compost

Figure 10.8 Onion growth test - the harvest on the right was grown in soil enhanced with toilet compost

Testing compost from a urine-diverting toilet

When the urine-diverting toilet is used, urine builds up in the urine chamber. A mix of faeces, soil, ash and leaves, builds up in the secondary composting unit. This final compost is rich in nutrients and also contains seeds which have passed through the alimentary canal. If the local diet includes tomatoes, then if this compost is placed in a container and watered young tomato plants will spontaneously grow (Figure 10.9).

Figure 10.9 Tomato seedlings

Figure 10.10 Young tomato plants

96 TOILETS THAT MAKE COMPOST

These may germinate in considerable numbers, but if most of the young plants are removed leaving the strongest two (Figure 10.10), the tomatoes will grow strongly using the nutrients contained in the bucket (Figure 10.11). Extra nutrients like diluted urine can be applied if necessary. The result of growing tomato plants in the urine-diverting toilet compost will be a healthy crop of tomatoes (Figure 10.12).

Figure 10.11 Tomato plants growing

Figure 10.12 Crop of young tomatoes

Growing trees in toilet compost

When an Arborloo is used the tree is planted directly in the toilet pit. But it is also possible to plant trees in toilet compost which has been excavated from a compost toilet pit and transferred to a hole dug specifically for a tree. The tree pit dug was 60cm x 60cm and 60cm deep (Figure 10.13). Toilet compost was dug out (Figure 10.14) and the tree pit was filled with the toilet compost to ground level (Figure 10.15). In this example, the toilet pit compost was excavated from a Fossa alterna pit after only 6 months of processing when it was not fully composted, instead of the recommended 12 months. However, the material was sufficiently composted to be easily transferred from the toilet pit to the tree pit.

Bricks were laid around the tree pit and the pit filled again with good topsoil (Figure 10.16). A hole was dug in the middle and topsoil added to the base of the hole. A young mulberry tree was planted in the hole and the soil levelled (Figure 10.17). Leaf mulch was then added and the tree watered. After four months, the mulberry tree showed excellent growth and was in

HOW TO USE TOILET COMPOST IN THE GARDEN 97

Figure 10.13 Digging the pit for the tree

Figure 10.14 Digging-out the toilet compost

Figure 10.15 Tree pit filled with toilet compost

Figure 10.16 Bricks laid around the tree pit

Figure 10.17 Planting a young mulberry tree

Figure 10.18 The mulberry tree after four months of growth

good health (Figure 10.18). As the tree grew, extra mulch and compost was added. Manure and other fertilizers can also be dug into the soil as the tree grows and requires extra feeding.

CHAPTER 11
How to use urine in the garden

Urine is a valuable supply of nitrogen, and also phosphorus and potassium in smaller quantities. It is particularly useful when used to enhance the growth of green vegetables, onions and maize. It can also considerably enhance the growth of fruit trees like banana and mulberry. Urine can be collected in bottles or from urine-diverting toilets. The following examples show what can be achieved by the use of urine application.

Crop trials using urine as a fertilizer

Rape

In Figure 11.1, the upper three basins of rape were fed 0.5 litres of a 3:1 water and urine mix, twice a week while the lower three basins received only water. The effect became noticeable after 10 days treatment and after 28 days of water and urine application the effect was very noticeable. Overall, rape yield was increased about 5 times by urine treatment (Figure 11.2).

Figure 11.1 Rape crop trials

Figure 11.2 Rape crop yields

Spinach

In Figure 11.3, the two columns of basins of spinach on the left were fed 0.5 litres of a 3:1 water and urine mix twice a week while the two columns of basins on the right were fed only water. The effective of the urine treatment is very positive and very clear to see. Overall, the spinach plants fed with diluted urine weighed 3.4 times more than spinach fed with only water (Figure 11.4).

Figure 11.3 Spinach crop trials   **Figure 11.4** Spinach crop yields

Mint and passion fruit

Mint and passion fruit also respond very well to water and urine treatment (Figure 11.5 and Figure 11.6). A weekly application of a 5:1 mix produces a significant increase in growth. This can be stepped up to two applications a week. Normally 0.5 litres of the mix per container is sufficient.

Figure 11.5 Mint after urine treatment   **Figure 11.6** Passion fruit after urine treatment

Onion

Some very good looking onions can be grown in cement basins with the help of a water and urine feed. Onion seeds are best planted early in the year, late January or February being good times, so they can be transplanted into containers towards the end of the rains in April. This healthy onion (Figure 11.7) was harvested in early September after six months of water and urine treatment in a 10 litre cement basin. An amount of 0.5 litres of a 5:1 mix of water to urine was applied once a week during the six-month period together with intermediate watering. Such a result reveals the usefulness of urine as a plant food.

Figure 11.7 A prize specimen of onion

Maize

Urine can have a significant effect on maize growth. In the fields urine can be applied straight to soil before planting in beds. It can also be applied straight in hollows made near the growing plant.

Maize is rarely if ever grown in containers, but the effect of the growth of maize in containers when fed urine is stunning and well suited for demonstration. Maize plants are hungry feeders and like a lot of nitrogen. The application of a 3:1 mix of water and urine, once or twice or even three times a week on maize, grown in 10 litre containers is particularly effective. Figure 11.8 shows the striking difference between a maize plant fed with a 3:1 mix of water and urine (0.5 litres) three times per week and maize irrigated with water only. Urine treatment also improves maize cob yield significantly. The total yield of cobs from maize planted in three 10 litre basins was dramatically different depending on how much diluted urine was used on the crop (Figure 11.9). Maize fed with 1750ml of urine per plant over the 3.5 month growing period resulted in a crop of 954 grams, compared with 406 grams for maize fed with 750ml of urine per plant, and only 63 grams for the maize irrigated with water only. These rates of urine application are quite high, but are happily accepted by the maize plants in the containers, which were irrigated frequently with water to keep the maize plants healthy. For small scale maize or sweet corn production, this method may have an application. It is also a useful way of demonstrating the effect of converting the nutrients held in urine into vegetative growth of valuable plants.

Figure 11.8 Maize fed with water only (left-side) and diluted urine (right-side)

Figure 11.9 Maize cob yields

Effect of urine use on maize growth on poor sandy soils: A field trial in Epworth near Harare

Epworth is a large peri-urban settlement of about 200,000 people close to Harare. It was chosen as an experimental site to demonstrate the effectiveness of urine as an alternative to commercial fertilizer for maize production because it is characteristic of the conditions under which millions of people live, both in peri-urban and rural areas in Southern Africa. Natural Epworth topsoil is sandy, porous, almost without nutrients and applied nutrients can easily be lost by leaching during heavy storms. Without commercial fertilizer or manure, maize and vegetable crops are generally very poor on soils of this type.

In the experiment, the field was dug and levelled beforehand and on planting day hundreds of small holes 30cm apart in rows 90cm apart were dug. A 20 litre drum of collected urine was shaken up and applied in 125ml amounts (Figure 11.10) to each hole. This was followed by a 500 gram plug of toilet compost. Two seeds of maize were planted in the compost and covered over with topsoil (Figure 11.11). If seeds are in short supply then a single seed can be planted. Over 90 per cent of registered maize seed will germinate. After germination 125ml of urine was applied at weekly intervals to each young maize plant (Figure 11.12). A crop of untreated maize shows the distinct difference in growth compared to the urine-treated maize (Figure 11.13

Figure 11.10 Measuring urine

Figure 11.11 Maize seeds planted on 11 November 2004

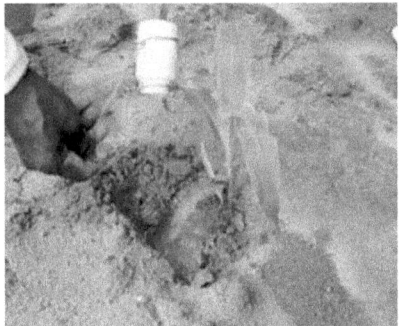

Figure 11.12 Application of urine to a young maize plant

Figure 11.13 Comparison between urine-treated (right-side) and un-treated (left-side) maize crops

Before applying urine to a maize plant, a small hole should be dug near to the plant (Figure 11.14). After applying the 125ml of urine in the small hole next to the plant (Figure 11.15), it is best to cover over with soil after application to slow down nitrogen loss. The total amount of urine added to each plant was 1000ml in eight doses of 125ml. After the initial dose, a dose was given weekly for five weeks followed by a dose every other week for the final two doses. The 1000ml of urine is equivalent to around 5 grams nitrogen, about the same as the dose used with commercial fertilizers.

Figure 11.14 Digging a hole for urine application

Figure 11.15 Applying the urine

Figure 11.16 First sign of tassel from 17 January 2005

Figure 11.17 First sign of the cob from 17 January 2005

After just over two months of growth, the first signs of the maize tassel and cob appear (Figure 11.16 and Figure 11.17). After two-and-a-half months, the growth of maize has been good and cobs are already forming. By comparison, maize planted at the same time but not treated with urine show smaller and paler plants with little cob formation (Figure 11.18). Overall, the application of 1 litre of urine per plant doubled the grain yield of maize growing on poor sandy soil compared to unfed plants.

Figure 11.18 Maize crop on 31 January 2005 – comparison of urine-treated maize (right-side) with untreated maize (left-side)

Effect of urine treatment on trees

Once established many trees can gain great benefit from the regular addition of the nitrogen and other nutrients in urine. Trees like banana, mulberry, mango and avocado are good examples. The addition of wood ash also helps to provide extra potassium which fruit trees need. The trees can also be fed with compost, manure or other fertilizers as they grow and require extra feeding.

Urine can be applied to trees directly from a urine-diverting toilet (Figure 11.19) or slowly through a hole in a bucket (Figure 11.20). Alternatively a hole can be dug next to the tree for water and urine application (Figure 11.21). In this case two litres of urine is added first (Figure 11.22), followed by ten litres of water. The technique works well on banana plants. In [insert Figure 11 23, the plant shown grew rapidly after the start of the rains and with the application of 2 litres of urine mixed with 10 litres water, twice per week. The bucket was fitted with a small pipe near the base to allow the water and urine mix to escape slowly into the ground (Figure 11.23 and Figure 11.24). This can also be achieved by drilling a small hole in the base of the bucket. Phosphate sediment will be leftover in the bucket and this is poured on the soil after the bucket is empty.

106 TOILETS THAT MAKE COMPOST

Figure 11.19 Urine applied to a banana tree directly from the toilet

Figure 11.20 Urine applied to a banana tree through a bucket

Figure 11.21 Preparation for urine application in a hole near the tree

Figure 11.22 Application of the urine into the hole

HOW TO USE URINE IN THE GARDEN 107

Figure 11.23 Bucket fitted with small pipe to apply urine

Figure 11.24 Inside view of bucket with pipe to apply urine

CHAPTER 12
Summary

This book has described the fundamental principles of ecological sanitation and provided a detailed description of how to build and manage a small range of lower-cost eco-toilets where the recycled products can be put to good use. Ample evidence has been provided for the value of both humus derived from human excreta and also the urine for enhancing the production of a range of food crops. The greatest effect is normally achieved by combining the use of both humus and urine. Methods of growing vegetables using recycled human excreta have also been described.

The techniques described here cover only a very small and as yet little known range of on-site options for lower cost sanitation. Many large-scale projects based on ecological sanitation are being undertaken around the world and these are receiving much attention. The techniques and methods described here are not as well known and are intended for use by poorer members of the community, who may in the past have used only the pit toilet or no toilet at all. However, it is this proportion of the world's population which is perhaps the largest, the least served and the most in need of improved facilities. It is hoped that this extended range of lower cost options will help to increase the coverage of this underprivileged segment of the population.

Ecological sanitation can also assist where people have used conventional waterborne systems like the flush toilet before, but where these systems are failing due to a lack of water or lack of maintenance of sewage processing systems. Overburdened or poorly maintained conventional sanitation systems can also pollute the environment considerably. These conditions apply mostly in the cities and peri-urban areas surrounding these cities. Where there is space, the systems described in this book may be useful. There are many projects currently being undertaken all over the world, where these same basic problems are being addressed by the application of ecological sanitation. GTZ and EcoSanRes are at the forefront of such work internationally.

There are a few central themes on which this particular approach to low-cost sanitation, described in this book, has been built:

- The toilet system itself must be thought of, not so much as a disposal system, but as a processing unit.
- Soil can provide the all-important link between the toilet system and agriculture. In the toilet systems described in this book, soil is added to the toilet in quantity – approximately equal to the volume of solid excreta added. And for best results, the added soil should be combined with wood ash and leaves.
- The added soil, together with its companion ash and leaves, converts, purifies and otherwise hastens the conversion of the foul and dangerous mass of excreta into humus, which becomes pleasant to handle, relatively safe and is rich in nutrients. The process is entirely biological, with beneficial organisms of all kinds tending to thrive and pathogenic organisms tending to die out. The inventor of the process is nature itself.
- The end result of this natural process is a valuable humus-like soil, which can be used to enhance the growth of both trees and vegetables. Excreta, soil, ash and leaves are abundant and cost nothing. In combination and when processed they have great value.
- The processing of human excreta, both humus and urine, is best integrated into a broader scheme of recycling all organic products in both the home and the garden.

Interestingly, this method of using soil to process human excreta was first used in the form of the 'earth closet' over 100 years ago. This technique preceded the use of waterborne sanitation as we know it today. The concept of using earth, rather than water, quickly went out of fashion after the invention of the flush toilet. As we have seen, the 'earth closet' and its variants still have considerable merit and greatly deserve revival.

All organic material can be composted. Thus leaves are recycled by making leaf compost. Organic vegetable matter, derived from both kitchen and garden, are recycled to make garden compost. Manure derived from animals is recycled to enter the compost heap. The composted materials from all sources, of both animal and plant origin, are applied back into the soil, which becomes enriched. Thus it is the combination of recycled leaves, manure, vegetable matter, kitchen scraps together with recycled human excreta which are used to form a medium which is mixed with topsoil to enhance the growth of food crops.

Put simply, eco-toilets form part of an ecological approach to managing the garden and home in a holistic way. Even used water – greywater – can be recycled in such a way that it can enhance the production of food. The home and garden becomes part of an eco-home and eco-garden. Recycling in all its forms is encouraged. That is how nature works!

The question then remains: what if I am not a gardener and have no interest or time to produce my own vegetables? Many may have no garden, but this will rarely apply to those for whom this book has been written. If this is the case, these eco–toilets will at least save water if the alternative is a flush toilet. If the alternative is a deep pit toilet, this new approach will provide an alternative facility which is safe, relatively cheap and pleasant to use. The fact remains that all pit toilets will eventually fill up and must be replaced sooner or later. For those millions who use pit toilets, low-cost eco-toilets may provide a good answer for the future. For many, it will be the low-cost of the simpler toilet systems described in this book which will have the greatest appeal. For others, it will be the ease of construction and the possibility of self sufficiency which will appeal. For others, the selling point may be that for the first time a toilet can do more than just dispose of excreta.

There is also the possibility that once put to use, the production of humus from the eco-toilet, together with the re-use of urine, may encourage the home owner to consider growing vegetables or enriching flower beds or growing more fruit trees. My own interest in gardening and the organic approach was much encouraged when I started to use an ecological toilet and reused the humus formed and the urine.

In this study I have been constantly amazed by the conversion process – how all these materials which in their prime state could never be classified as soil – easily turn into a product which can only be described as soil. Thus leaves turn into soil, organic wastes from the kitchen turn into soil, vegetable and manure turns into soil and even human excreta turns into soil. Soil is surely the beginning and the end of it all. In this discipline, the answer does indeed lie in the soil.

But even the richest soils need rejuvenation when they have yielded their nutrients up to the growing plants, and a method of constantly re-introducing the nutrients derived from urine and humus into the soil is required. Thus compost or processed manure should constantly be introduced into the vegetable garden. Where jars, basins or other containers are used, once the vegetables have been harvested, the used soil can be tipped out into a pile, sieved and introduced into a fresh pile of soil to which fresh compost or eco-humus is added. So there is constant rejuvenation of the soil which is used.

And careful use of both organic and even inorganic plant foods, even those available on the market, can also be used carefully in combination with the methods described.

CHAPTER 13
Conclusions

This book attempts to provide practical information which will allow those living in rural, peri-urban and even some urban areas of Africa to build and practice the art of recycling nutrients from their own excreta in order to gain better crops and vegetables in their own back gardens. The work is primarily intended for use in East and Southern Africa (Figure 13.1), where there is space, where backyard gardening is practiced and where the climate is warm and wet seasons are interspersed with dry.

Figure 13.1 Eco-toilet in Ruwa, Zimbabwe

The basic principles outlined in this book are the most important. These principles can be adapted to suit local conditions in various countries in the sub-region. The method chosen will depend on several factors, not least the amount of money available to build a facility and the willingness of the user to engage in the practice of recycling.

It should be remembered that all these eco-toilet systems require a degree of management which is far more demanding than required by users of the normal deep pit latrine or even the flush toilet. This may not always be clearly understood at first. Thus practical hands-on training and demonstration are vitally important. Often judgements about final design and processing methods may be taken only on-site where soil type, ground stability and drainage have been assessed.

The methods described in this work represent new ventures into the world of low-cost sanitation, and there is still much to learn. This work has been written by a researcher, who dabbles at the fringe of understanding. There is an ocean more still to learn. The methods described are intended to add on to the sanitary range of options already available and not compete with them. The pit latrine, currently the commonly used excreta disposal system in the world, has survived over the centuries because, alongside its potential deficiencies, it has great merit. It is simple and easily managed. A pit dug 3m deep may take 10 years to fill and thus requires limited management. When full however, the pit is usually difficult to empty and a new toilet must be built. The pit toilet can also be upgraded with a screened vent pipe to make it almost odourless and fly free. In the great majority of cases pit toilets do not seriously pollute ground water, especially if the toilets are well placed in relation to the water source, about 30m distant. However, in high density settlements where pit toilets are built close together and shallow wells provide a source of domestic water, contamination of the water source is possible and even likely. This is where shallower pit or urine diversion eco-toilets can play a useful role.

The flush toilet and related waterborne systems have brought with them the possibility of people living together in cities, and of greatly reduced incidents of disease which has made modern life possible. Thus the application of waterborne systems made possible a huge rise in living standards for countless millions of people around the world, and this continues to be the case. All sanitary systems have their place. Both the pit and flush toilet systems will remain as major excreta processing systems for as long as we live. They will be joined by urine-diverting systems and variants of both the flush and pit toilets which make recycling possible. There is room for all these systems to be used in the most appropriate setting.

This new ecological approach to sanitation has come just in time to add a new perspective and dimension to sanitation itself. The low-cost alternatives described in this book offer truly practical solutions for providing acceptable sanitation on a small budget. Very often it is the simplicity, low-cost and ease of construction which may appeal at first to the beneficiary, and upgrading from one system to another is always possible over time. The direct link to agriculture and forestry is also an important element in this new initiative. The additional benefits of recycling the compost and urine to enhance food production and tree growth are clear to see. These various practical benefits may convince the householders to take up the ecological approach to sanitation by building a compost toilet. Only time will tell!

Bibliography

This book is an abbreviation and simplification of the longer 'An Ecological Approach to Sanitation in Africa' (Peter Morgan, 2005; updated 2006) where the following books and references were used.

Andersson. I, with Esrey, S., Hillers, A., and Sawyer, R. (2000). *Ecological Sanitation for Food Security*. Publications on Water Resources No. 18. Sida.
Austin, A. & Louiza Duncker (2002). Urine-diversion ecological sanitation systems in South Africa. SCIR. Pretoria, South Africa.
Balfour, E.B. (1943). *The living soil*. Faber and Faber. London.
Barrett, M., Nalubega, M., & Pedley, S. (1999). On-site sanitation and urban aquifer systems in Uganda. *Waterlines*. Vol. 17. No.4. 10 - 13.
Benenson, S. (1990), *Control of Communicable Diseases in Man*. Fifteenth Edition. American Public Health Association, Washington.
Breslin, E. D. (1991). Introducing ecological sanitation: Some lessons from a small town pilot project in Mozambique. Paper presented at Stockholm Water Symposium, Sweden.
Breslin, E. D. & dos Santos, F. (2002) Introducing ecological sanitation in northern Mozambique. Field Work Report of WaterAid. London.
Bromfield, L. (1949). *Malabar Farm*. Cassell & Co. Ltd. London.
Carson, Rachel. (1962). *Silent Spring*. Penguin Books Ltd, Harmondsworth. England.
Clark, G. A. (1997). Dry sanitation in Morelos, Mexico. *Ecological alternatives in Sanitation*. Water Resources Publication No. 9. Sida, Stockholm.
Del Porto D. & Steinfield. C. (1999). *The Composting Toilet System Book*. Concord USA. Centre for Ecological Pollution Prevention. pp. 234.
Devlin, J.F. & Zettel T. (Eds), (1999). *Ecoagriculture: Initiatives in Eastern and Southern Africa*. Weaver Press. Harare.
Epstein, S. (1995). *Growing fruit trees*. Forestry Commission, Harare, Zimbabwe.
Eshius, J. & Manschott, P. (1978). *Communicable Diseases. A manual for rural health workers*. African Medical and Research Foundation. Nairobi.
Esrey S.A., Gough, J., Rapaport, D., Sawyer, R., Simpson-Hebert, M., Vargas, J., Winblad, U.,(ed). 1998. Ecological Sanitation. Sida. Stockholm.

Esrey S.A. (1999). Nutrition - Closing the Loop. *Proceedings of the Workshop on Ecological Sanitation.* Mexico. October 1999.

Esrey S.A. & Andersson, I., (1999) Environmental Sanitation from an Eco-Systems Approach. *Proceedings of the Workshop on Ecological Sanitation.* Mexico. October 1999.

Feachem, R.G., Bradley, D.J., Garelick, H., & Mara, D.D., (1983). Sanitation and Disease: Health Aspects of Excreta and Wastewater Management (London: John Wiley).

Gao, XZh, Shen, T., Zheng Y., (2002) *Practical Manure Handbook.* Chinese Agricultural Publishing House. Beijing.

Gough, J. (1997). El Salvador experiences in dry sanitation. *Ecological alternatives in Sanitation.* Water Resources Publication No. 9. Sida, Stockholm.

Hills, L. D. (1981). *Fertility Gardening.* Cameron & Tayler. London.

Hopkins, D.A. (1945). *Chemicals, Humus and the soil.* Faber and Faber Ltd. London.

Howard, Sir Albert, (1943). *An Agricultural Testament.* Oxford University Press. London.

Howard, G. (1999). On site sanitation and groundwater: The art of balancing unknown risks? *Waterlines.* Vol. 17. No.4. 2 - 5.

Jenkins, Joseph, C. (1994) *The Humanure Handbook.* Chelsea Green Publishing Co. PO Box 428, White River Junction, VT. USA.

Jönsson H. (1997) Assessment of sanitation systems and reuse of urine. *Ecological alternatives in sanitation.* Publications on Water Resources. No.9. Sida. Stockholm.

Jönsson H. Stenström TA, Svensson J. and Sundin A. (1997). Source Separated urine - nutrient and heavy metal content, water saving and faecal contamination. Water Science and Technology, 35 (9).

Manson. T. (1975) *Tom Manson's New Garden Book.* Pioneer Head (Pvt) Ltd. Salisbury, Rhodesia.

Manson. T. (1991) *Tom Manson's Garden Book.* Roblaw Publishers, Harare, Zimbabwe.

Ministry of Water, Lands and Environment (Uganda). (2003).Directorate of Water Development. South Western Towns water and sanitation project. Ecological sanitation design and construction manual.

Morgan, Peter R. (1990). *Rural Water Supplies and Sanitation.* MACMILLAN. London.

Morgan, Peter R., (1999). *Ecological Sanitation in Zimbabwe.* A compilation of manuals and experiences. Vols. 1, II, III and IV. Aquamor Pvt. Ltd. Harare.

Munkhondia, T. (2003). Quarterly report on the CCAP Eco-sanitation project at Embangweni, Malawi.

Saywell, D. (1999) Pollution from on-site sanitation - the risks? what risks? *Waterlines.* Vol. 17. No. 4. 22 - 23.

Simpson-Hebert, M & Sara Wood, (1997). *Sanitation Promotion Kit.* WHO. Geneva.
Simpson-Hebert, Mayling. (2006). 'Ecological Sanitation: A CRS Ethiopia Success Story'. *Report posted to the EcoSanRes discussion forum on Yahoo Groups 11 Dec. 2006.*
Smit, J. (1999). Integrating Urban and Peri-urban Agricultural and Urban Waste Management. Proceedings of the Workshop on Ecological Sanitation. Mexico. October 1999.
Steinfeld, Carol. (2004). *Liquid Gold. The lore and logic of using urine to grow plants.* Green Frigate Books, Sheffield, Vermont. USA.
Stenström, Thor-Axel, (1999). Health Security in the Re-use of Human Excreta from on-site Sanitation. Proceedings of the Workshop on Ecological Sanitation. Mexico. October 1999.
Stenström, Thor-Axel, (2001). Reduction efficiency of index pathogens in dry sanitation compared with traditional and alternative waste water treatment systems. Internet Dialogue on Ecological Sanitation (15 Nov. – 20 Dec. 2001).
Strauss, M. & Blumenthal U. J. (1990). Use of the human wastes in agriculture and aquaculture - utilization practices and health perspectives. IRCWD, Dubendorf, Switzerland.
Sykes, Friend. (1946). *Humus and the Farmer.* Faber & Faber Ltd. London.
Tompkins, P. and Bird, C. (1998). *Secrets of the Soil.* Earthpulse Press. Anchorage, Alaska.
Vinnerås, Björn, (2002). Possibilities for sustainable nutrient recycling by faecal separation combined with urine diversion. PhD thesis. Swedish University of Agricultural Science. Uppsala, Sweden.
Winblad U. & Kilama W. (1985) *Sanitation without water.* MACMILLAN. London.
Winblad U. & Simpson-Hebert M. (Editors). (2004). *Ecological Sanitation –* revised and enlarged edition. Stockholm Environment Institute.

www.ingramcontent.com/pod-product-compliance
Ingram Content Group UK Ltd.
Pitfield, Milton Keynes, MK11 3LW, UK
UKHW021834140426
5217IPUK00021B/1445